ARCTURIAN STAR CHRONICLES

VOLUME TWO

Intergalactic

Seed Messages for

the People of Planet Earth

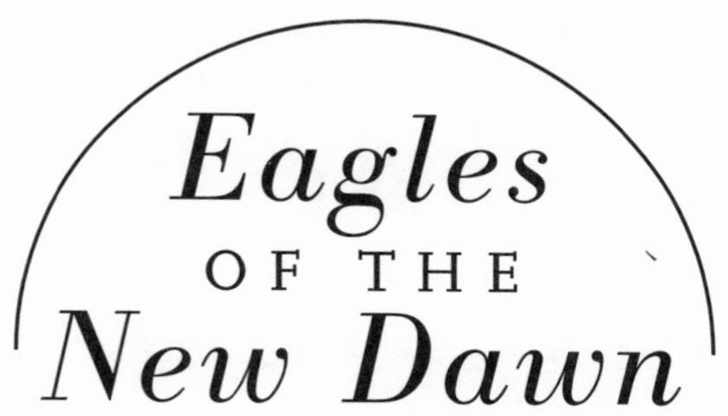

A manual to aid in understanding matters pertaining to personal and planetary evolution

---

Patricia L. Pereira

Beyond Words Publishing, Inc.
20827 N.W. Cornell Road, Suite 500
Hillsboro, Oregon 97124-9808
503-531-8700
1-800-284-9673

Editor: Sue Mann
Composition: Rohani Design
Cover printer: Phoenix Color
Proofreader: Marvin Moore

Printed in the United States of America
Distributed to the book trade by Publishers Group West

Library of Congress Cataloging-in-Publication Data

Pereira, Patricia L.
Eagles of the new dawn / Patricia L. Pereira.
p. cm. — (Arcturian star chronicles ; v. 2)
ISBN 1-885223-59-5
1. Human-alien encounters. 2. Telepathy. I. Title. II. Series:
Pereira, Patricia L. Arcturian star chronicles ; v. 2.
BF2050.P46 1997
133.9′3–DC21 97-17957
CIP

The corporate mission of Beyond Words Publishing, Inc.:
Inspire to Integrity

For Patrick and Sharon

Table of Contents

Part II

Messages for Evolving Humans

Interlude

Greetings from Tashaba

Part III

Escalating Songs

Part IV

Introduction to Malantor

Part V

Childhood's End

Appendix

Personae

THE ARCTURIANS: Fifth- and sixth-dimensional beings of light from Blue Crystal Planet in the Arcturian star system (also called the Boötes system). The handle of the Big Dipper points directly to a bright star, which is Arcturus. One of the "jobs" of the Arcturian star council is to serve Spirit upon the Supreme Hierarchical Council for Planetary Ascension, System Sol. Base of operations: Saturn.

MALANTOR: Creator of melodious lyrics, Arcturian poet, and intergalactic star councilor-teacher on Earth assignment. Masculine vibration.

PALPAE: Arcturian galactic envoy, Ambassador of Light, Love, and Peace, Intergalactic Brotherhood of Light to people of planet Earth. Preparer and sealer of documents. Patricia's primary spiritual guardian. Masculine vibration.

Quaker: Arcturian "seed planter." Greeter of newly established human telepaths. Door opener. Masculine vibration.

Quantra: Arcturian solar scientist. Guides and directs flows of energy that emerge from the radiance of the sun(s). Harmonizes webs of the stellar grid. Solar-body essence. Masculine vibration.

Quoarts: Arcturian lunar scientist. Guides and directs flows of energy emitted by moons. Moon-body essence. Feminine vibration.

Tashaba: Catlike entity from the Sirian star system. Serves upon zoo (or ark) ship. Gathers DNA and spirit essence of Earth's endangered and extinct species for future retrieval upon Earth or for return to stars of origin. Feminine vibration.

Introduction

I was forty-eight years old when I became aware that I am telepathically connected with extraterrestrials from the Arcturian star system. In retrospect, I remember a night when, as a child of seven or eight, I awoke to a crackling sound emanating from the basement of my home. Tiptoeing to the top of the stairway accompanied by our Doberman pinscher, I peered down at a light as bright as the noonday sun. The house appeared to be on fire. Instead of crying out to my parents, I just stood there with my quivering dog. I clearly remember calling out, "Who's there, who's there?" Then I went back to bed. I never spoke of the event until recently. As a young teenager in the early 1950s, I was walking home from church one star-tossed evening pleading with the night sky, "Come help us! Come help us!" I now know a part of me has always realized we are not alone.

I always had difficulty saying the word *God.* I felt embarrassed, ashamed. What I was taught by my church made God seem small, demanding, vindictive, and contracted. I decided that I must be an agnostic, perhaps even an atheist. Searching for mental, emotional, and spiritual satisfaction, I began to study world history and the philosophy of the Greeks, Germans, French, English, and Americans. Then, in the early 1980s, I was invited to a question-and-answer session with two very aware spiritual teachers, Sharon and Patrick O'Hara. Moments into the evening, all my doubts and frustrations slipped away. Instantly, my life changed. I began to meditate in earnest. Expanding my philosophical studies, I explored Native American spirituality, Buddhism, Hinduism, Taoism. Time with God and serving God became the primary focus of my life.

In the transformative year of 1987, the year of the Harmonic Convergence, I was a divorced medical transcriptionist who had become infatuated with the issue of reintroducing wolves into the Yellowstone ecosystem. A few years earlier, I had started an environmental educational organization in Boise, Idaho—the Wolf Recovery Foundation. Though busy with all the details of running the fledgling foundation, I set aside time each day to meditate upon spiritual matters. One sunny June morning, I happened upon a copy of *With Wings As Eagles* by John Randolph Price. He suggested that if one wants to channel, one simply sits quietly in meditation and records what comes. As I did so, I became immediately aware of word thoughts drifting lazily through my head that seemed different, but yet similar, to mine. I wrote word after word. When I was finished, I thought, What gibberish, what nonsense. A few days later, I read what I had written and discovered I had composed a poem, "Give Honor to Your Dark Side," which is in the beginning of this book.

I thought, This is pretty amazing, and I decided to give it another go. Instantly, I received the transmission "Greetings." I "heard" a happy, chuckling sound inside my head that identified itself as Quaker. I was puzzled; what was this? A few days later I experimented again and was introduced to Palpae. I was told that Palpae is an entity from Arcturus whose body is made up of light substance. Palpae is my main contact, my mentor, my constant, thought-connected companion. Soon I began to look upon Palpae as a wise, gentle, loving father figure.

Palpae and the Arcturians I communicate with hail from the fifth and sixth dimensions. The star Arcturus and her planets form a multidimensional solar system. To locate Arcturus in the night sky, find the Big Dipper. The handle points directly toward a large bright star. That shimmering star is Arcturus.

We who reside in the slower-vibrating third dimension experience our bodies and the world as physical matter. The fifth- and sixth-dimensional Arcturians, however, live upon planets that vibrate, not as physical matter, but as light. My understanding is that a dimension is like a musical octave. Earth vibrates slowly and is a heavier octave or dimension. As a planet begins to refine or quicken its vibration, it becomes lighter and lighter until, eventually, it moves up the scale into the adjoining octave or dimension.

I am told that, in our universe, for every physical planet there are at least four or five light-substance planets.

Because of my increasing connection, I became interested in the phenomenon called channeling. I found that the well-known channels of the day—Knight, Pursel, and the like—are primarily trance channels. That is to say, consciousness leaves their bodies while entities speak through them. Others do automatic writing, their hands moving as if by themselves.

It seems to me that with the upgrading of energies upon the planet, channeling is evolving. Since 1987, I have met many people who are quite consciously aware that they are telepathically connected to spiritual beings from various dimensions. I believe that each of us, in our own unique, creative way, will one day be consciously connected with Spirit. One purpose of these collected writings is to assist you in unlocking the doors of your mind to the majestic spiritual worlds.

When I connect telepathically to other dimensions, I must always know where I am tapping into. Entities who reside in the lower domains of the fourth dimension (called the astral plane) can be quite manipulative and controlling. Twice in my early weeks I failed to "hook up" properly, and extraterrestrials commonly referred to as the Grays invaded my mind. The experience was upsetting and quite frightening. I quickly learned to check my sources. I discovered that certain words or phrases contain highly refined vibrations that cannot be used in telepathic communications by negative-oriented beings. Though not always included in the written transcripts, the greeting "Hum of the many planets" or the salutation "Adonai" immediately assures me and identifies my level of connection.

In his initial transmission, Palpae stated, "Please understand that our language and yours are not synonymous. We will attempt to communicate with you in overtones that are equivalent to your personal perception of language." Many times I have had cause to reflect upon these lines. English is one of the most difficult languages for expressing spiritual concepts. For instance, the beings with whom I am in contact always refer to themselves as "I/We." It is the clearest way to describe an individual who is in constant harmonic communication with Cosmic Mind, That Which Is One. However, to make reading this book easier, I decided to use "I" when the being communicating refers to himself or herself, and "we" when the being refers to Arcturians or other galactic species in the collective.

The Arcturians use many descriptive terms to identify God. Their purpose is to expand our perception of God, the universe, and Self as Soul (a spiritual being cloaked in a physical form). Additionally, they refer to Christed Energy as Sananda, or the Essence. Christ is defined by Paramahansa Yogananda in *The Divine Romance* as one who "rose above ordinary human consciousness and entered the cosmic Christ Consciousness, the pure reflection of God present in all creation." The Arcturians recognize Christ Consciousness as one who has incarnated upon Earth many times to serve all humanity, not only as Jesus, but also as Krishna, Buddha, Lao Tsu, Moses, Mohammed, Quetzalcoatl, and the Dawn Star, among others.

The primary purpose of these essays is to acquaint you with principles of Universal Law and to introduce you to our brothers and sisters from the stars. The writings contain information to prepare us for galactic citizenship. The Arcturians remind us of our collective role as planetary stewards and of our responsibility to interact in a peaceful, loving, protective manner with all of Earth's life forms. They want to expand our perceptual horizons until the energy we now expend focuses upon our inner lives as Soul in service to Greater Good, or God.

In closing, I would like to devote a few moments to thank the people who have supported and encouraged me over the years to persevere, until 1994 when I connected with Cynthia Black and Richard Cohn, the visionary owners of Beyond Words Publishing, who courageously challenged themselves to publish this manuscript. In particular, I want to thank my spiritual sister Clare Heartsong; Barbara Eddy, for being my creative mentor and inspiration; Linda Erickson, for her early editing efforts; my husband, Clifton, for his loving steadfastness; my beloved spiritual teachers, Patrick and Sharon O'Hara; and special thanks to my editor, Sue Mann, for her attention to detail and perfectionism, and for preserving the integrity of the work.

Statement of Purpose for Earth Visitation

Arcturian Contingent, Intergalactic Brotherhood of Light

We, who are of the Arcturian contingent, Intergalactic Brotherhood of Light, announce our presence before humankind. Hear us, people of Earth, for we have come to acquaint you with the processes of planetary evolution. Our purpose is to invite you to the stars. Our purpose is to awaken you to the experience of God's living presence as the focal point of your daily lives. Our purpose is to guide you in unlocking and accessing the dormant functions of your minds.

Welcome us, for we are of your family. We have come to prepare you for the greatest event in Earth's history.

Within the realms of present-day scientific knowledge, there is little that concurs with our methods; however, know that Earth is in the midst of an evolutionary event: the transposition of her material body to that of the essence of Spirit. Note well that the procedures and ramifications involved in the transformative process are manifesting galaxywide as well as within your planetary home.

Within this manuscript we will endeavor, as simply as possible, to refocus the priorities of your lives.

There will come a number of entities onto these pages. The majority of us hail from the Arcturian planetary system, although among us many star complexes, galaxies, and even universes are represented. Our emissaries stand ready to greet you. Eventually, you will come to recognize us all, for you are our lost brothers and sisters.

We serve under the auspices of Earth's Spiritual Hierarchy.

Give Honor to Your Dark Side

Give Honor to your Dark Side.
Honor the reflection of self in the eyes of another.
Use this experience to walk a path of wisdom,
to grow,
to release your self-imposed
traditions of the past,
outmoded ways of acting,
of perceiving and believing.
All that you wish to be free of is inside the Self.
Look at these things.
Honor them for their gifts to you.
Then, let them fly from the wings of
your consciousness.
Let go. . . .
And thus,
Travel to the stars.

The Initial Song, June 1987

Prelude

Palpae, as part of the telepathic mind of the Arcturian galactic envoy to planet Earth, sends greetings. We have traveled over vast distances of interstellar space to salute our brothers and sisters of planet Earth. For many, many aeons beings of light from the stars have observed your world, and the plains of Earth are rich in clues that speak of our presence.

Evolution's hour has arrived; the time is ripe for this generation of humans to awaken. In the early years of the coming century, the time for the starships' subtle maneuverings will end. The men and women of Earth will find themselves conspicuously introduced to beings of light of the Intergalactic Brotherhood and the coordinating councils that oversee your solar system's spatial quadrants.

As humans began to develop a taste for living in a state of obscure autonomy at a very critical juncture in their prehistory, they decided to reject even the slightest hint of interference in their private affairs by outside forces. It was at that time that the Memories, which their conscious minds once held of the worlds of light, became lost to all but a very few. Paradoxically, humans concurrently came to the conclusion that they had been left to fend for themselves. As the sorrow of loneliness overcame them, they became enmeshed in the webs of spiritual sleep.

As immature humans ventured forth to discover their new world, they gradually became consumed by and fascinated with their biological urges as well as intoxicated with the sweet taste of acquiring objects. As they became increasingly distracted by the majestic beauty of Earth and more delighted with the pleasures of the physical form, the Memories began to fade more rapidly. Because humans generally neglected things of the Spirit, the knowledge the ancient ones had openly shared with them in the years of innocence was withdrawn and buried until such time that the awakening ones began to mature.

In this introductory segment, I will explain how and why the person who has recorded these writings was chosen to consciously interact with the beings of light. This entity's—Patricia's—life has seen much struggle, and her pathway to the Memories has wound like a snake slowly making its way over rock-sharp terrain. If you correctly intuit your heart's emotional responses to the paragraphs of this narrative, your essence will begin to clearly comprehend the many ways you resemble this simple woman who found herself conscripted quite abruptly into the Arcturian galactic light forces to serve as a telepathic energy receptor and transmitter.

If you were to come upon Patricia, you would not easily recognize the power and heat that has been granted hers to emanate; indeed, she herself is quite unaware of the depth of its magnitude. She is surrounded by many people who would never presume to consider her private activities, those moments when she makes herself available to the communicative thoughts of extraterrestrial beings. How could this woman have logically reasoned that one beautiful summer's day in her life's middle years, as she began to experiment with writing the softly forming words she heard drifting through the back of her mind, she would find herself startled by the presence of a telepathic energy laughingly calling himself Quaker? How could she know that this essence would shortly be replaced by the resonant vibrational hum of a being who Patricia would soon come to know as her special star guidance counselor, Palpae of Arcturus, who introduced his substance as a being whose purpose is to serve the people of planet Earth as an ambassador representing the multidimensional Intergalactic Brotherhood of Light?

Why, then, was Patricia contacted for this assignment, and not yourself?

Although it is true that the preparation of this manuscript is Patricia's challenge to perform, the talented gifts of all spiritually evolving humans are of great import in aiding aspects of planetary evolution. In fact, you are all encoded with a personal matrix of information that is poised, ready to activate the expression of purpose into your daily lives. Spinning and spiraling, the DNA helix impregnates the tissues and membranes of your bodies with genetic data that contain all your minds need to access the finer vibrating hum of the light worlds. Like threads caught up in Creation's robe, cords of pure light insinuate themselves into the emotional fibers of your hearts, assuring the eternal *you* integral positions in the cosmic design.

Purpose arises out of Love's perfect energy. Purpose unfulfilled is like a patiently smoldering ember. The spark of spiritual passion applied to the human intellect is the kindling that sets the flames of purpose blazing. One's inner fire then erupts as a burning desire to intimately serve God—the Omnipotent One.

The longing to fulfill one's higher purpose is an acute and chronic desire that permeates the core of a being who is serious about personal spiritual transformation. The awakening ones are among those who incorporate within their emotional fields an intense yearning to transcend the pervading ennui of third-dimensional spiritual sleep.

The transmissions from Patricia's pen incorporate within them certain energy themes whose patterns are especially designed as a series of primer informational packets. It is my pleasure to scatter symbolic word pictures before your eyes like seeds sown upon fertile ground.

To encourage the germination and maturing of humanity's return to innocence, and with the specific permission of the star councils, Patricia has been directed to modify, simplify, and clarify the solar-to-Earth data-disk transmissions that make up her manuscript within the limitations inherent in human communication. Therefore, this book is an experiment that transcends the idea of channel.

These essays are a co-creative work. They are written by Patricia in close companionship with and in observational monitoring of all data by beings of light that counsel her.

Patricia's first consciously stated intention to commit her life in service to the Absolute took place several years prior to that afternoon in 1987 when she abruptly found herself face-to-face with extraterrestrials. While performing tai chi, which she believed capable of sustaining heightened energies within its yielding patterns, she clearly and somewhat forcefully transmitted her emotion-filled pledge and called upon That Which Is to assist her. Unaware that she had been born with the specialized talents peculiar to a high-velocity solar-star-connected telepath, the power of the transmissions issuing from her mind reverberated through the ethers like thunder following a bolt of lightning. Engulfed with an energy that flooded over her like waves coming from the sea while evoking her personal image of God to hear her, she dedicated her life to serve that which Spirit willed of her.

It was not long after this episode that Patricia suddenly found herself consumed with the desire to participate in bringing a healing upon a species of animal that resonated with the same hum as her beating heart: *Canis lupus*, the wolf. To this day, Patricia's intellectual self cannot rationally or logically explain to other humans the single-minded passion and unwavering determination that in midlife suddenly overtook and possessed her. Her almost instantaneous devotion to an animal she had never seen was so intense that it elicited a courage from her never before hers, a force so empowering she found it within her ordinarily shy and private self to stand before strangers to teach them and share with them the beauty and majesty of the animal. Not content to rest, she wrote reams of letters to many people and formed an organization so that others whose hearts smoldered with love for the elegant creature might come together to accomplish a mutual goal. Thus, this woman earned and was granted the right by the star tribes to use the title Manitu (spirit keeper) as if it were her name.

I have encouraged Patricia to share this aspect of her life's story to enable you to comprehend more clearly that within the regions of your hearts a great passion also lies buried. I would have you understand that the *you* whom you are is an essential cog in Creation's wheel. The people who are fully cognizant of the magnitude of their human potential are few; for the majority, absolute self-knowledge lies hidden within the recesses of their hearts.

Seek! Seek that which is thy greater Self!

As a whole, humanity is in a state of great despair. The men, women, and children of your planet are quickly losing hope that they will ever make right that which most profoundly torments them. Although we do not suggest that you put aside all you possess to accomplish the highest purpose for which your particular self was fashioned, we do recommend that you closely observe the rituals of your daily life while you endeavor to enhance awareness of your higher Self until you are adept in interpreting its whispers. How magnificent it would be if all humans were to set aside a minimum of an hour each day to actively participate in some form of practical or ceremonial healing beneficial to themselves, their fellow beings, and Earth as well.

Are you one who has put your relationship with the Creator on the back burner of your life's interests, and do your personal disappointments and sorrows seem just too much to bear? No matter the predicaments of your life, deep within you carry an innate knowledge of the profound. There, hidden in the subconscious, you remember the universe.

Come. Learn to concentrate your energies. Endeavor to walk the sacred, spiritual path. Focus your mind and emotions upon Love's rhythms only and, in spite of yourself, you will begin to sparkle like a living rainbow. Surely then your day's load will become lighter. Remember, these are magical times!

Resolve to take your place among those who are earnestly and courageously working to ease the stress that, by necessity, accompanies a major shift in the polarities of a planet's vibratory hum. Become one with those who are the pioneers of the new dawn.

One cannot escape noticing the deterioration of human society, the rampant erosion and decay of the inner cities, and the grave ecological backlash resulting from overwhelming worldwide environmental pollution as well as ongoing massive deforestation. I will mirror our views to you as might a guest coming into your home whose eyes are greeted by a residue of dust and grease clinging to the surface of your finest crystal and china. Correspondingly, I will emphasize that as the awakening humans flow ever further into the energy fields of Love's radiant Oneness, they will inevitably begin to transpose the growing planetary wastes into a flowering mecca.

To merge with the higher vibrations that are the true influence behind planetary affairs, it is not necessary for you to be politically influential, to have great wealth, or to possess the noble stature of a renowned religious, political, or financial figure. You need not loudly reverberate like a boisterous strummer before whom young people swoon. As a consciously evolving being who is committed to spiritual Self-discovery, your inner light will naturally shine as brightly as a star. Earth, gentle, startled reader, is calling you. In the next years it will be the great unnoticed, those humans who are the fibers upon which society is hung, who will be the ones who are instrumental in precipitating massive cultural, environmental, and spiritual change.

So, how do you find your place and begin to transform a troubled world? Simply. Find a moment (and the courage and resolve as well) one day to telephone or write to your government's intrepid leaders. State clearly that you, as a citizen, petition them to demonstrate a greater regard for that which you cherish. Encourage them to serve their bewildered constituency in such a fashion that privately and publicly they will represent the highest ethical and moral ideals. Attend a gathering of like-minded people, those who share common problems or interests, who meet to embrace and comfort one another with words that elicit encouragement and love. Create an atmosphere of cheer and goodwill at your place of "busy-ness." When all is in chaos, laugh and smile and refrain from spilling the beans behind another's back. Become an island of peace in a sea of turmoil. Then, as night stretches her shadows, enclose the hands of your children within yours and remind them of their relationship with the angels. Do not let your children forget the knowledge of pure innocence that was theirs at birth.

The essays of this manuscript contain a multitude of complex sentence structures; however, the basic intention behind the messages is quite simple: We would teach you to Love. We would have you experience Oneness as the natural state of your conscious being.

Additionally, we will represent ourselves in such a manner that the fright you normally experience when confronted with the realities of the "unknown" dissipates until it no longer holds fear's power over you. We are well aware that if a multitude of metallic-appearing starships were to suddenly materialize in the skies over your cities, such an event would serve no purpose but to startle and place fear's images before you.

Though this manuscript certainly is not our initial attempt to contact humanity, it has been compiled in such a manner as to awaken you consciously to our presence and to acquaint you further with the nature of our beings. We have found that the most beneficial method of announcing our intentions toward the species *Homo* is through the energies of creativity: music, film, paintings, literature, and the like.

People of Earth, you are our Oneness, you are our stellar family. You and we are not unlike a single cell in Creation's living body. May your loneliness slide comfortably away as you slowly realize that you are on the road to the stars.

What a sight, as we observe our awakening brothers and sisters and prepare your seats before the feasts of the universes!

The sparkling lights of the stars are calling you. Read further and come to know of us. These pages will acquaint you with beings of light who ride upon the starships. The essays will acquaint you with the sky warriors, or the eagles of the new dawn, our human and animal ground forces, who are dedicating their lives to actively participate in the cosmic evolution of Earth, their planetary home. Among these beings are men and women very much like yourselves. In time, you will come to a complete understanding that the tie binding humanity to the stars is a linkage that has never really been broken.

As swallows fly on summer winds, you soar now, ever closer, on an unrelenting course whose destination is the stars.

This is our prelude. This is our song. A field conduit of light energy are we. Sweetly we sing for your delight.

Part I: Eagles of the New Dawn

Definition

Palpae

Eagles of the new dawn are those who consistently focus upon fulfilling the purpose their Souls came to Earth to perform, whose conscious intention is to incorporate spiritual wisdom into their daily lives. Dedicated to following Spirit, they naturally radiate unconditional Love-Light energy, which stimulates a natural healing of Earth Mother, plants, and animals.

Eagles of the new dawn will create a sustained peace from the ashes of worldly chaos. Visionaries of the new dawn, their dedication to Spirit will be instrumental in facilitating far-reaching evolutionary changes. Their etheric bodies wing high in the planetary ethers where, with all-encompassing eyes, they scan the farthest reaches of heaven and Earth, for they have discovered cosmic truth.

People of Earth, open your hearts wide, for the residual members of human society, those who focus attention upon serving God, are about to manifest the stuff of their dreams into the airy fortresses of reality. You who choose the stars will attain them much quicker than the bulk of humanity ever dared dream. Initially, you will access the stargates in the meditative state. However, as your vibrational rhythms soar, a time will come when your physical bodies will dissolve into light and you will float about as light as air. You will achieve planet liftoff with dovelike ease. A time will come when the star navigators residing within your hearts will traverse the oceans of space without maps and you will have instantaneous access to all galactic ports of call.

I am in attendance upon you this early morning's light. May these small groupings of words in some way bring encouragement to a forlorn people.

A poem

QUANTRA

You are in pain and you lose hope
whenever you give priority
to the things of humanity
before honoring the things of Spirit.
Then, mournfully, you walk down life's long highway.

Gently allow the hidden recesses of your mind to open
as softly as the budding petals of a newborn flower.
May Love's delicate radiance shine
like a brilliantly lit golden orb
through all that you think, say, and do.

Quiet your emotional yearning.
Your grief-filled thoughts are as transitory
as the autumn winds.
Listen instead to the hum
of Spirit's magnificent song.

Are you not gloriously alive?
Envelop yourself in Earth's majesty.
Sing ecstatically!
Are you not bound in Oneness with
Omnipotent Universal Spirit?

Let go of sorrow!
Let go of loneliness!
For the stars dance and beckon to you
from around future's bend.

Your body's toils will dissipate soon enough,
fading like dust into a forgotten past.
Your Spirit-Self is eternal;
cosmically wise, all-knowing Soul.

You have been apprised of these things untold times.
There is no thing to fear!
You always experience God's vibrations
whenever you make a choice for Love.
Would we deceive you?
We, who resemble starlight
and the hum and glory
of the many suns?

Rest peacefully, human sisters and brothers.
Allow Love's healing rays to envelop you.
Remember, you are God's beloved children!

Essays

QUANTRA

Omniscient knowledge in all star systems is stored in cosmic libraries located within each system's sun(s). Earth's sun, Sol, is the "central computer" for your planetary system. Raw thoughts telepathically generated by spiritually immature minds are filtered through Sol for vibratory refinement prior to being absorbed by our minds.

Purified knowledge contained within solar libraries is accessible to spiritual seekers. Upon request, the awakening are granted admission to this sacred information. As you begin to stretch inward intuitively and telepathically, you will eventually find yourselves exploring the contents of the brilliant archives that make up your solar library.

As you become aware that you are naturally telepathic, you will realize that thought is a mighty tool and a powerful, unlimited energy source. Indeed, Light-Love energy eternally radiating from Supreme Omniscient Mind is the impetus or primal cause from which all matter is created.

This essay is meant to set the gears of your mind spinning. However, a detailed description of the nature of suns is not the purpose of this essay. It is meant to tantalize and awaken your dormant Soul Memories.

With their vibratory hum sufficiently modulated to third-dimensional level, fifth- and sixth-dimensional starships may suddenly appear in the skies above Earth as rapidly spinning silver spheres. However, the Intergalactic Brotherhood's starships are not formed of metal, but are thought-generated into vibrant form. They are products of our creative minds. Cooperating as One we mold the contours of our ships around pivotal hubs of naturally formed crystals. Our thought in combination with energy the crystals emit supplies our fuel "tanks" with unlimited power.

Crystals have been placed upon Earth as tools to assist your spiritual awakening. Eventually, crystals will provide you with an uncontaminated, purified, perpetual energy source—not granite, not wood, not metal, not electricity, and certainly not petroleum or nuclear fission. Humankind, you have missed the point! You have always missed the point. Now you are coming very close. Nevertheless, you still miss the point.

Palpae

While you investigate the contents of our star-to-Earth transmissions, take careful note of any corresponding thoughts and emotions they trigger. As you begin to trust the integrity of your expanding frame of spiritual reference, your physical bodies will begin to vibrate refined light. Eventually, the time will come when you will know without a doubt that you are formed from intelligent energies that constantly emanate from the imaginative mind of Omniscient Creator.

Flows of time are rapidly propelling the "present" into the "future." What once was experienced as linear time seems almost nonsensical as humanity's unencumbered, erratic thoughts catapult Earth into the opening layers of the fourth-dimensional space-time continuum. The minds of the awakening are saturated with mystical visions of ancient civilizations, long-buried continents, planets of far-distant suns, and brief glimpses of outlandish-appearing universes.

Your body's vibratory rate will elevate when you incorporate recommendations telepathically received from the Love-Light realms into your daily routines. As your cellular matrices refine, they begin to radiate positive thought emissions beneficial to Earth, other humans, animals, plants, and even spirits floundering in the lower fourth-dimensional (astral) regions. As you awaken, you begin to initiate a process of spiritual evolution in preparation for ascension from the third-dimensional realms into the harmonics of the refined vibratory octaves.

In peace we come as One. We are pure Love essence in accord with Prime Star Maker. Our thoughts transmit unqualified joy's boisterous energies, unqualified ecstasy.

Quoarts

As you move into a role of planetary caretaking, you may feel compelled to focus waves of loving thought in the moon's direction whenever a new moon is born. As the moon plods silently along her orbit she cries hungrily for a return of the ancient ones, the time when a simpler people attended her special needs with rituals, singing, and dancing. Now few remain who honor the moon ceremony arts. Contemporary humans are not aware that low-voltage lunar energy from time to time requires an energized charge from high-wattage thought. Concentrating loving thoughts directly at the moon supplements her subtle light emissions with a high-octane boost of purified Love-Light energy. But to adequately perform the simple details of lunar "housekeeping," you must carefully plot the optimum time by studying the moon's phases.

Illustrious lunar wisdom is contained within the core of Earth's august celestial companion. Similar to information stored within the sun, the moon houses data related to Earth's position within the harmonic grid that attaches Earth and the moon to other planets within your solar system.

Scented whiffs of space poppies emitted as starship residue connect nutrients of flowers and waters to space and sky. As they pass through the ethers cavorting like whales dancing among sea urchins, starships emit tinkling crystalline sounds that complement, attune, and stabilize harmonics of the planetary hum.

As we observe awakening humans refine the details of their spiritual ceremonies, our moods take on an ecstasy of wonder, for what we observe is quite magnificent. Your loving thoughts and purity of intention are so sublime that they evoke our deepest emotions. Spiritually hungry, you yearn for God. Ah, you radiate exquisite light!

Palpae

A new dawn is emerging upon planet Earth. You who are endeavoring to co-create with Spirit in these transitional times are layering Love-Light energies within Earth's body that, like granite stones, comprise the building blocks of a magnificent future. The loving works you perform enhance the ability of your star family to swiftly incorporate harmonic alignment among Earth, her moon, and other solar bodies.

As you awaken, try as you might you will never be able to return to your "old stuff," nor will you wish to. Your commitment and dedication to spiritual growth will cause you to shine like a beacon of light. Encourage others as well to walk the high road. Courageous are you who step forward upon the sacred path that culminates in spiritual evolution. When you become dis-couraged, remember that Earth's fate rests in the capable hands of the Christ Essence and the Spiritual Hierarchy. As you open your heart to embrace their teachings, you will be filled with light to a degree you never before experienced.

May you travel tightly held in hope's warm arms, for beings of light from the starry realms are always with you. You are our beloved brethren, and you are on the road to

Celestial Home. It serves no purpose for you to shake, rattle, and roll in fear. (Laughter is discerned.) We, too, delve from time to time in the realms of humor. It is a common imperative throughout the universe—that a joyful sound transmitted as laughter is infectious and is an emollient that soothes cellular manifestations of dis-ease on many levels. A display of goodwill and fellowship among humans is paramount to integrating life-force energy during these transformative times. Become aware of the quality of your endeavors and the many instances when your participation with others plays a key role.

In the near future humans will be forced to acknowledge the presence of extraterrestrials on Earth. You must understand that there are both negative and positive components to extraterrestrial activities. When meeting these beings we advise against hasty judgment calls as to the nature of their spiritual development.

Prior to any such meetings, however, it is important that galactic-aware individuals respond with love, trust, and a positive approach toward Earth's future. We would appreciate your cooperation and compliance in this regard.

As you accept that all humans are, by nature, multidimensional telepaths, you will progress to a point when you recognize that your thoughts perpetually blend with Universal Mind. Eventually, thought integration between us will be easily accomplished. Knowledge gained in the process will enhance your awakening and recognition of universal truth.

We urge you to hesitate negating your spiritual experiences and truths as you understand them because of fear, feelings of doubt or unworthiness, or the opinions of the less enlightened. Negative, fear-based emotions are not compatible with a positive flow of Love-Light, fundamental Prime Law energy. As you evolve, you will recognize that humans are about to accomplish what they have spent many generations attempting to achieve.

Patricia, I closely observed the weakened energies you exuded during your early years. I watched as, almost single-handedly, you attempted to uncover truth's essence by forcing yourself to study reams and reams of obtuse history and philosophy of Western culture. Year after year you diligently devoured book after book. Taunted and half-frustrated, you teased yourself with page after page of writings replete with dark images, superstitious half-truths, and human misunderstandings. Nevertheless, you persevered. For many years you gathered only the seeds and husks of truth's ripe fruits, unaware of the treasures that awaited you. However, the day finally arrived when you reached a point of greater awareness. At last you comprehended the simple truth: Divine Knowledge is an energy force manifesting as Love-Light and all things in the physical universes are structured upon the creative powers inherent in Prime Law.

Moment to moment, day to day, and year to year you have spent your life searching, always searching. I observed as you almost forcefully wrenched yourself into a place of slowly dawning awareness. But even in moments of grave self-doubt, your fundamental beliefs were never truly challenged. Never have you succumbed to the temptation to surrender the validity of what you have intuitively recognized as truth since childhood. In reality you fought only to comfortably mesh your logic-oriented brain with what your heart-mind has always known to be true. Now you clearly understand that the foggy visions which once tormented you served only to separate us and you in your mind. Now you not only recognize your celestial family but the humans who make up your Soul family as well.

Most of you welcomed our arrival long before your logical minds acknowledged our presence. As children (even as adults) you cried out in your slumbers for our return. Brothers and sisters of Earth, soon we will assume a place of Oneness returned; what you view as imaginary will soon mentally correlate with your visionary, antediluvian Memories.

Humans, you are the spirit of our dreams, as we are of yours. May we gather together as One, for the returning will soon be upon us. We stand ready to welcome you aboard the intergalactic starships.

Quality work is laid down. As she transcribed thoughts to paper, Patricia's and our thoughts merged in Oneness; abundant joy radiated from Patricia's heart-mind. Understand how closely the telepathic process binds us. Unification of spirit is a basic characteristic of Universal Mind. Almost effortlessly, practiced human multidimensional telepaths perceive that which is "us" and that which is "them" to be highly intimate, for telepathic experiences speak of no separation. Then they begin to comprehend that a bonding of we-you radiates Love-Light magnitude energy.

Do not suppose, you who rapidly shift from peace to various manifestations of sorrow, that it ultimately matters if you allow your ego to be caught up in the temptation to practice perpetual self-other torment. When you indulge in the tricky illusionary vagaries common to third-dimensional beings, you are simply allowing your smaller self to settle for a limited vision of your greater Self. At such times you are failing to put into practice the basic fundamental of Universal Law: to apply Love's essence in daily life. Your penchant to critically judge yourself and others is a rather nasty habit of your temporal ego and certainly not something that emanates from your divine Self.

Pestilence so pervasive is on Earth. On a variety of levels, it affects all the other planets and their satellite moons. This pestilence, your warlike manipulative behavior, has severe ramifications throughout your entire solar energy sector. Light emissions arising from Earth are essentially devoid of high-wattage Love energy. Fear-laden, you pulsate destructive energy into the cosmos. Spinning like whirling dervishes, your devilish thoughts finger their way into Earth and into neighboring spatial realms. Uneven sparks of disruptive negativity stream outward into galaxies far beyond the Milky Way.

Such willful attitudes and self-indulgent behavior are luxuries you can no longer afford. If you desire to sustain yourself as a life form upon vibrationally refined Earth, it is imperative that you learn to activate and use Love-Light energy in everything you think, say, and do.

But many of you have come to realize that a state of chronic dis-ease seriously plagues your sun system. Because of your growing awareness, you have committed yourselves to playing a critical role in environmental healing and in restructuring the planet's light grids.

Tashaba

Trapped as you are in the dense vibrations of the third-dimensional hum, you may attempt to give yourself completely to others. But sometimes you will experience the unpleasant sensation of being dropped like a hot potato. Such irrational conduct is not in accord with beings of light who travel in God Oneness. Therefore, programmed into this informational primer are techniques to aid you in maintaining spiritual awareness.

Fifth- and sixth-dimensional beings of light do not lose one another in the sense humans do when they must let go of those they love because life circumstances or death's illusion separates them. Although we perform a multitude of independent functions, our beings mutually intertwine so that Oneness is our constant experience.

Humans who perceive Oneness as being limited to sexual coupling are basically lonely people. The intermingling that we experience is not to be confused with tactile, physical sensation. Our expression is of simultaneous energy bonding both inwardly and outwardly, in a manner altogether inexplicable to humans. Our beings are maintained in constant union with one another, and we never suffer from pangs of loneliness. That which is termed *apart* is an unknown for entities who have evolved to light-body status. Nor is it a hardship or sacrifice for us to leave our home suns and travel from star to star. Quite wonderfully, our ships are living extensions of all that is familiar to us, all that is radiant Love-Light. In the gentle arms of the Ab-Soul-Lute we travel lightly held. Our expression is that of Creator's essence. We are fully cognizant of our connection to an abundant, vital universe.

PALPAE

Beings upon the flowered starships predict that a series of tragic events, triggered by unstable emanations from the minds of evil-oriented people, await humankind. These things will be a prelude to sorrow that in interludes will build to a crescendo before the new age is born. To protect yourselves during these difficult times, learn to observe your ego self with a clear eye. The future for the spiritually astute will be wondrous beyond humanity's greatest expectations, so learn to cooperate with directives received intuitively from your inner guides. Commit and recommit to serve in God's holy ranks. We recommend a carefully balanced diet of ecstatic anticipation mixed with large doses of positive attitude. Such a diet will nurture your spirit and preempt disharmonic thought forms when they attempt to entice you off your path.

Eventually, you will discover you have integrated the higher teachings at all physical, mental, emotional, and spiritual levels. Then you will understand that no thing occurs haphazardly and that all things are in a state of perpetual being with That Which Is.

The Arcturians

We encourage you to approach the following essay as if it were written just for you. The emotional and mental distress Manitu puts herself through is a commonality shared by most of you. Humans who view themselves as being of greater or lesser worth than others put their spirits in the distressful situation of diminishing, degree by degree, the power of their light-body wattage—an unnatural expenditure of essence energy.

A good day to you, Manitu. Though in the initial phases of your evolution as a telepath you had only a vague sense of what was truly transpiring between us, you frequently pondered upon your star-based family. Soon you became aware that the visions which have always ebbed and flowed within the quiet recesses of your mind depict real events, places, and beings. As you began to peek through your mind's hidden corners, you discovered new ways to approach your outmoded way of thinking. Prior to consciously connecting with us, you were already learning to overcome your tendency to rationalize what your intuition or heart-mind knew to be true. Because of rigid thought moldings imposed upon your mystical mind by a logic-limited educational system, you found it very difficult to conform. Eventually, as you learned to trust your Self's greater knowledge, you became comfortable with your natural inclination to embrace a cosmic-based philosophy.

However, we must caution you, you have given almost all your hard-earned green rectangles and energy to Greater Cause. Frantically, you attempt to mold your chaotic financial life into some sort of order that will comply with what is necessary to maintain your basic needs while you attempt to serve without qualification what you believe in your heart to be what God asks of you. In so doing, you have discovered how very difficult it is to live a purely spiritual life when caught within the confines of an industrialized society.

Life has been your greatest teacher, has it not? Now you clearly perceive the dichotomy between humanity's plan and Creator's plan. There seems to be little enough money or energy for your will to serve in perpetual accordance with Prime Will. Faced with the grim possibility of a shelterless existence, you sometimes feel you will have to put aside what higher worlds envision for you in order to honor the things of human society.

Manitu, you have not even begun to fathom the depths of the abilities that sleep within you. Because you have never perceived yourself as harboring special talents, you have never really contemplated your full worth. When you were younger you viewed yourself as more or less inadequate. Is this not true? Gently, we admonish you to remember that all beings are integrated Oneness with God. Do you suppose you reside on a level different from universal unity? To believe so is a reverse "ego trip." Diligently you attempt to free yourself of such entanglements. In so doing your physical energy is often tremendously reduced. Through our eyes, however, you have become aware of your ability to radiate refined light, and you hold yourself proudly before Prime Creator with no cause for apology. Can you honestly state that you do not serve God adequately? Does not your Soul's beauty shine from your eyes? Why do you persist in viewing yourself as being of lesser stature than those you deem eminent or successful? However, you give yourself credit for the pleasure you receive when tending to the everyday tasks that enhance the lives of those you love.

The joyful performance of self-other needs—the cooking, cleaning, picking up, and other service-oriented functions—fall into the category of greater Soul purpose. Indeed, when routine tasks are performed with an intention of integrity, one is in cooperative mode with Creation's plan for humanity.

We have taken you severely to task, star daughter. Yes, we do understand that sorrow, pain, and fear play dominant roles in most human lives. Yes, we do understand the difficulty of being confronted by people who view themselves as being of elevated station. The perpetuation of better-than or lesser-than ideology throughout human history is a primary reason the Intergalactic Brotherhood continuously scrutinizes Earth's energies. Negative-projected emotions and their thought forms are naturally debilitating to the vital forces of people, plants, and animals. Fear-based vibrations escaping from the collective human mind form shadowy substances in the astral worlds where lightless figures float incessantly, attaching themselves like cancerous cells to the planetary grids and to the outward flow of the interspatial grids.

On a higher note, we know that efforts made by all human telepaths when thought-addressing the star fleet are a shining example of the abilities lying dormant in all of you. We are aware of all who devote time and energy to protect and dispense interstellar information entrusted to their care. In time, a doorway onto the golden streets of a dawning new world will open before those of you who have dedicated your lives to interact with beings of light who serve Prime Creator. We bestow our gratitude upon those who fearlessly assimilate extrasolar data. You who hold faith and trust as to what can be accomplished by beings who dwell within starships will see. Yes, very soon you will see!

Ponder deeply upon our remarks! Ego enhancement or ego loss is one of the most objective indicators of overly delicate human psyches. Individuals wishing to attain fifth-degree vibrational status would be wise to energetically neutralize all negative-radiating energy that lies within their emotional and mental bodies.

We are the Arcturians. For the purpose of enhancing the mind-meld we transmit in vibratory unison. We will guide and counsel Manitu because her name is scattered to the winds as "one of those loony women who talks to little green men." We know she happily accepts this small inconvenience.

We are exceedingly proud of the courage displayed by all humans who, with insightful open-mindedness, are answering the call to actively interact with fifth- and sixth-dimensional beings of light during these accelerated, evolutionary times.

Palpae

One late evening, Manitu's etheric body was brought aboard the starship *Marigold–City of Lights* as an honored guest of an auspicious star council session. A congratulatory tableau was played by the galactic chorus in recognition of the co-creative service she willingly performs in harmony with the Intergalactic Brotherhood of Light. Honored was she by the Christ Essence, Sananda, He to whom she sweetly sings in her heart's depths.

It is virtually impossible to transport a third-dimensional being's cellular matrix intact into a fifth-dimensional craft without an extensive organ-by-organ vibratory "remodeling" prior to the exchange. Therefore, human starship visitation is accomplished by raising the etheric, or spirit, body into the vessel. The human's experience is that of an intense, realistic (but dreamlike) out-of-body episode.

We realize that many are reluctant to accept as a possibility such a wondrous thing as spontaneous interdimensional travel for humans. Nevertheless, we are pleased to inform you of the ease of its accomplishment. Indeed, a great many who wish for such an event are often observed wandering freely in their dream bodies, exploring our magnificent starships. Your individual will predicates our decision to activate a visitation upon you; we trust you are aware of this stipulation.

Manitu has discovered that she is often witness to activities upon starships but that she does not always remember her visits. Not unlike most of you, she expected that sensations associated with such an event would be quite dramatic. However, she finally concluded that boarding the starships and meeting extraterrestrials face-to-face are rather ordinary experiences. Though she is unable to explain the details of these events in a manner acceptable to the scientific community, nevertheless, her growing state of spiritual clarity has shown her the reality of her paranormal experiences.

We have introduced into this primer extrasolar documents translated into English, anticipating that the suggestions they contain will help you assimilate spiritual practice into your daily lives. As you are aware, focused attention upon higher knowledge (as you perceive it) connects your consciousness in alignment with Infinite Mind.

It does not matter what path you choose when you are intent on knowing God. Within the heart-minds of all people, Creator resonates as Prime Omnipotent Source. Higher states of being do not recognize differentiation in truth. A tendency toward separate thought processing has convinced humans that the wonders of applied Universal Law as Love-Light cannot be easily accomplished.

As you gain a greater understanding of our extrasolar teachings, your bodies will begin to resonate at a refined frequency and you will automatically incorporate features of the Law of One into every aspect of your lives.

We suggest that you ponder upon the deeper significance of our statements.

Part II: Messages for Evolving Humans

Opening Remarks

Palpae

All over the world, plants and animals that live near humans are refining their minds to act in accordance with One Mind. These wild ones intuitively recognize that Earth's harmonics are in a state of evolutionary transition. Judiciously maintaining separation from chaotic humanity, they have always merged their cellular rhythms with Earth Mother. Their thought energies drift like soft downy feathers upon awakening human minds.

Heavy of heart, humans walk the lands. The magnitude and degree of their grief escalate. Yet the enticement of perpetual peace, tenuous though its melodies, is heard faintly humming throughout the prairies, mountains, and oceans that make up Earth's broad vistas.

The capsuled moments you call time quiver and vibrate as Earth's vibrations refine. Those who honor Universal Law swim rapidly for a brilliant-lit shore where delicately hued starships await them. Wondrous beings, those whose lives are dedicated to seeking and serving Divine Principle, will, one fine day, join their brothers and sisters from the celestial domains.

Some humans are deceived by the tricky vagaries of material-based society. They allow the demands of the temporal world to take priority over their spiritual needs, which puts their Souls in danger of falling prey to the evil intentions of repugnant beings who inhabit the astral nether regions. Surely they slide toward a yawning abyss, which will receive their spirits into shadowy lands. Though it is not too late to catch the upswinging tides that lead to the angelic realms, the opportunities to do so diminish.

A Brief History of Planet Earth

The Arcturians

As Earth was cooling, a group of deleterious beings from many systems arrived upon the planet and attempted to stake a fraudulent claim upon her. When starseeds arrived to colonize the newly blooming planet, a mixture of positive-negative energies (Souls) settled on her body. From these nefarious beginnings a *Star Wars*–type scenario erupted. Many skirmishes have been held throughout Earth time, and the battle has swayed back and forth for millions of Earth years. You who live in current time are witness to the erupting of endings, for those who have held Earth captive are being moved to the interior of a spatial region far beyond human perceptual fields.

Arcturians have been monitoring Earth for five million years, since the original Arcturian starseeds were laid down upon her. We will not attempt to replay the history of these events in this limited document.

Arcturus is one of many star systems that have had an impact on Earth's development. Most often we act as a harmonic unit to perform a variety of functions. For example, Arcturians, Pleadians, Sirians, Lyrans, and some evolved aspects of Orion have always been there. To perform certain functions we will, at times, incarnate as humans or animals. However, our doings are only a small sampling of the activities that take place around Earth.

Earth's unique environs are particularly interesting in that her inhabitants require a great deal of constant attention. Because of the instability of dark versus light that has been occurring for millions of years in your solar system, the star councils remain alert. The "commander in chief" of the star councils is the Christed Energy, sometimes referred to as Sananda. Various orders of light brotherhoods of ascended and embodied masters, angelic beings, and spiritually advanced extraterrestrials (the Intergalactic Brotherhood of Light) are united in Oneness to aid the people of Earth in removing the dense cloud of fear and negativity that Dark Lords have tied about the planet body.

Does your education system suck the juices from your Souls? Indeed. Separation of church and state sees to that. But in countries where church and state are combined, we see restrictive doctrines and practices rigorously maintained by religious orders and governing bodies. Retention of power has long been the main game on your planet. The only hold Dark Lords have over you is when they convince you that you are not in or of God. Thus we lay bare their trap.

Because of the early negative-positive energies settling upon Earth, she was set aside as an experimental station for ripening species and for alleviating the cosmos of unruly fragments. At one point the Spiritual Hierarchy and Dark Lords agreed to a truce, and they decided to establish Earth for multisystem use. This truce has been broken many times. After the fall of Atlantis, Dark Lords captured and enslaved the planet for the purpose of "energy mining." That horrific situation continues in present time.

Dark Lords have used various devices to instill fear in the populace (human and otherwise), among them conflict and agitation-based decision making, grappling and devouring each others' bodies to sustain physical form, and instilling a false sense of time by the simple act of dividing *now* into three parts—past, present, and future. The latter was instrumental in flushing out all vestiges of alignment with Oneness, which is the true ripeness of being that characterizes civilizations who make up the galactic core.

As the illusion of linear time settled upon you, folds of gravitational pull intensified until it became impossible for you to access your escape pods and achieve liftoff. Thus have you been held in confinement, mostly by the bonds of Orion.

Earth is by no means the only planet where this situation exists. The question, at this point, becomes too complicated for clarity. We ask that you absorb that which is given. We will add that the entire Sol system was drawn into battle. That which is termed the "asteroid belt" between Mars and Jupiter was once a planet of incomparable beauty, thrown asunder in the early years of battle. That which is Mars, after a time of cooperative peace, became a holding point for negative energies. That which is Venus remains a planet of exquisite jewellike higher-dimensional beings who grace this sun system with intelligence far beyond the concepts humans can understand. (They are quite amused by your innocent probes into their third-dimensional space.) Indeed, that which is the Order of Melchizedek Light Brotherhood originated on Venus and came to Earth to serve its unfortunate human brethren in slipping off the confinements that had subjected them. The work of this high brotherhood order remains in place today and is directed from Earth station Shambhala. Shambhala is located in the spatial planes of the Gobi Desert and is one of twelve cities that exist in Earth's etheric regions.

That which came to pass cannot be placed as blame upon Earth species. You are victims of a holy war between beings of light magnitude and beings of dark magnitude. You have been separated from us for so long you can scarce recall us.

You are living kindred spirits with the star system of your personal allegiance—perhaps Arcturus, Sirius, Pleiades, or the Andromeda galaxy—and you are kindred spirits with all beings who inhabit Greater Cosmos. From the core of the Central Sun our Souls marched forth to inhabit this grand universe. Indeed, you have lived many places and have seen the rise and fall of many suns. That which is your human self is a microcosm of who you truly are: Soul.

You must realize that Earth is a spatial battleground. Earth serves as a training base for advancing Souls. Earth is a penal colony for wayward energies. Earth is a prisonerof-war camp for both positive and negative forces. Earth is a primary school, a teaching planet for Soul evolution.

We have attempted to outline millions of years of complicated Earth history and multisystem-multispecies interaction as simply as possible. Now we must let you draw a few conclusions. Think, awakening masters. Think: Allow your Soul Memories to unfold.

An addendum. The Arcturians are here to protect our precious starseeds. We are here as warriors of the light. We are here to set teachings of a profound nature into and upon the planetary soils so that humans may arrive at a point of awakening. We have participated with several other systems (notably the Pleiadians) to set holy teachings in all human cultures. The holy, sacred scripts are actually cosmic teaching manuals.

Primarily we are here in service.

Expanded Thoughts on Telepathy

PALPAE

To correctly interpret the subtle messages that float before your mind's quiescent eye, to fluently communicate with fifth- and sixth-dimensional beings, you must first establish clear telepathic linkage. Novices at the subtle art of voiceless communication, you must learn to discipline your uncontrolled thoughts and master pinpoint concentration. As you advance in your ability to communicate telepathically and evolve spiritually, you will be permitted access into the refined octaves. Your natural aptitude to exchange thought spontaneously will then accelerate. Eventually, you will discover that you need exert only a whiff of energy to instantaneously transmit and receive information with beings of light.

With little effort an evolved mind can instantaneously transfer large blocks of data as one unified energy field, thus freeing the sender to focus upon other endeavors. The receiving mind functions in a similar manner. Stored transmissions may be retrieved whenever circumstances deem it appropriate, particularly when multidimensional data are to be received by a human channel. Simply stated, incoming blocks of information are held in space storage, not unlike a telephone answering machine that retains a message until the receiver accesses it.

Undoubtedly, as you peruse these data on telepathic communication, your initial reaction will be one of impropriety or intrusion. We are not unaware that you may feel as if your thoughts had tumbled out for all to see, that your innermost being was suddenly and obscenely exposed.

Clearly, and with the utmost regard for the sensitivity of your position, we reiterate: One of the most pervasive illusions perpetrated upon humanity by Dark Lords—those evil, manipulative, controlling beings—is to support the widely held belief that thoughts are private and can be seen and reviewed only by one's self. Graciously we remind you: Vibrationally refined citizens of the great star nation are all adepts at telepathic communication. Thought is energy, not some intangible substance whose contours are contained within the bones of your forehead.

If you consider transdimensional telepathy a rash invasion of your right to privacy, if you feel that you no longer have a comfortable, secure place in which to hide, we offer little to encourage you. On the other hand, if you ask someone who routinely channels multidimensional beings of light, you will discover that telepathic encounters with beings who are in service to Divine Oneness transcend the warmest human relationships. Being saturated with an effusion of soft, glowing, loving acceptance and freedom from fear is a natural extension of ethereal-to-physical thought exchange.

From time to time we enhance the energies of our telepathic relays with one another so we may achieve direct conversation with specific humans. Those of you who have dedicated yourselves to living life's greater purpose are automatically granted celestial guidance and are, therefore, under surveillance by beings of light who serve Divine Will. Also, those who hold positions of authority within the world's institutions, those who make decisions that critically affect humanity and Earth's environment, are thoroughly scrutinized. High-ranking government and military figures, executives of megacorporations, economic leaders, and the scientific elite are among those monitored. Those whose intellectual or spiritual wisdom (or lack of same) places them in positions of teacher, counselor, priest, and the like are particularly susceptible to extrastellar observation.

The human mind is not unlike a searchlight arcing through the night sky. Pulsing like beams of flashing light, electrically charged sparks are constantly emitted by the neural synapse centers of Earth's thought-evolving creatures.

When learning to communicate telepathically, you must routinely challenge the Love-Light intention of all incoming energy. Clearly state your reason for establishing contact with multidimensional beings. Limit your thought communiques to entities who radiate high-frequency emissions, those who resemble starlight. You will know them by the quality of their Love-Light radiance.

If any anxiety persists during telepathic encounters, it is quite possible you have contacted lower-world, negative-charged entities like Dark Lords. If you feel even the slightest disturbance with the contact, immediately disconnect from the telepathic wave by replacing all negative mental and emotional influences with quality images radiating Love-Light.

As an Arcturian ambassador from the Intergalactic Brotherhood of Light to the people of Earth, it is my assignment to soften the mental and emotional barricade that humans' fear-laden, suspicious natures have erected between them and the magnificent inhabitants of the great star nation. The greatest obstacle that divides us is not constructed of space or time—it is woven from the fabric of human thought. The closed recesses of cosmically dormant human minds have always limited their ability to access the universal language of the stars.

I bid the sweet energies of peace to settle around you.

Comes Palpae of rosy red Arcturus. Allow your visionary eye to settle upon an image of rainbow-hued, crystalline starships. You who seek to have the honor of spiritual dignity restored, reach out with your minds to the occupants of the ships and greet them as you would any well-known acquaintance.

The nature of telepathic communication eliminates the need to be in the right place at the right time, such as when you use a telephone. Therefore, communiques slated for transmission to Earth can be stored until the time is appropriate for humans to bring them into form. This is particularly true of written material, which often originates as a cooperative effort among several minds blending as one mind.

As Patricia became aware, as she grew in knowledge of the intricacies involved in star-to-Earth voiceless exchange, she arranged to record transcriptions at her convenience. We are most appreciative of the adjustments and sacrifices human channels make to fit multidimensional communication into their busy schedules.

When we decide to send data, we accumulate them and then, affixing energy to a receptive human mind, release them into the ethers. Prior to mingling thought with disruptive energies that flow around Earth, however, we often modulate extrasensitive transmissions by sending them backward through crystalline field transformers in the Pleiadian star system. Thus, sometimes transmissions arcing Earthward from Arcturus are transmitted via the Pleiades. The Pleiadian star fields are ideally suited for transmitting energies Earthward from many sectors of the galaxy.

The Pleiadian star fields are used another way. Because mental energy tends to move in a circular or spiraling manner, before highly charged human negative emissions surge outward onto the delicate space grids, they must be safely deflected. For this purpose, silo-shaped crystalline towers were long ago erected on several Pleiadian planets to capture and refine energies erupting from your sun system. These massive crystals transmute the more rebellious energies. When they are revitalized, they are returned to Earth.

Energy and Crystals

Quantra

Waves of massive, dark cloudy images spread like an umbrella over Earth's face. To offset eruptions of these potentially volatile energies from destroying her, and to refine these energies, instruments similar to Pleiadian crystalline towers are on our starships. Shipboard personnel focus beams of light upon wayward incoming transmissions and deposit them into the crystals. The energies are absorbed and treated by blending them with rainbow-hued light, soothing melodic sound, and sweet floral scent resembling lush flowers.

We also circulate positive-charged light strands between starships and strategically placed pyramids planetwide. Whirling rods of unstable energies are neutralized by "computerized" lasers that capture, cool, flush, and refine them before they can shoot their negative-based emissions onto the light-sensitive space cords. Like surgeons who have assortments of surgical tools for extracting diseased organs from their patients' bodies, we solar physicians maintain a variety of devices for healing and repairing distressed areas within planetary bodies.

Patricia found this information difficult to receive, and we do not doubt it may be equally difficult to comprehend. However, in these data are important references to our self-sustaining power source. To illustrate: Starships are propelled by crystals impregnated with a mixture of thought, delicately hued light, sweet melodic sound, and a subtle hint of essence of rose.

It is not a difficult thing for us to activate the power that resides in naturally telepathic crystals. Beings who thought-communicate recognize that the ability to transfer and receive energy is inherent in all matter. Everything, every substance, is capable of thought. Every molecule of every planet and its minerals, plants, and animals; the moons; the stars; and the ethereal wisps that bind the universes in Oneness are energized by Love-Light—the intelligent, creative force of Omnipotent Mind.

From a human perception, the materials that make up Earth's geologic structures appear solid and incapable of movement. In actuality, rocky matter is formed of ethereal light. The grids that make up Earth's spiritual body resonate Source Mind as Love-Light, as does each mote of dust. Each minute portion of universal "stuff" vibrates sustained patterns of God's omnipresent thought.

We suggest you build upon the concepts many of you hold regarding the properties contained within crystals and gemstones. Humans are naturally drawn to their radiant beauty, but few understand their true purpose. To expand your knowledge of the symbolic nature of crystals, meditate upon emeralds and view them as containing lush forests teeming with animals. See rubies as repositories of dusky sunsets and brilliant sunrises. We could discourse in depth on meditating upon crystals and gemstones, but we suggest you use this exercise as an excellent way to flex your intuitive muscles. Begin by pondering upon the luminescent characteristics of milky white pearls.

Crystalline melodies are soft and sweet, not unlike the hushed tones of a lullaby. Few recognize that your fascination and love of gemstones and crystals go beyond appreciation of their intrinsic beauty. Once you knew your crystalline companions well, and joyously you laughed and played together as One. Now the crystals are calling you Home. Like Pied Pipers summoning children, their delicate essences beckon and urge you to awaken.

We encourage you to observe yourselves and your planet as if you were seeing from our viewpoint, that is, from a higher-resonating dimension. For now, we bend a loving salute to you; we greatly sympathize and understand the intensity of your human struggles.

Spiritual Awakening and Galactic Participation

Palpae

If you diligently seek us, you will find us. Nightly, the starships sparkle splendidly, radiant colors flashing in front of the stars. Remember, we do not go where we are not invited. You must be one who seeks beauty, who hungers for God, before you are awakened to our presence.

As the light grows, the eyelids of the spiritually arousing begin to flutter. Like newborn babes gasping for first breath, vibrationally refining humans are beginning to view their world as if seeing it for the first time. Filled with hope they wave welcome to the cloud-cloaked ships hovering above Earth's cities. Succulent as ripening oranges, as sun-warmed apples in a summer's orchard, are your thought responses to the beings of light who inhabit the starships. In reply, we return an ecstatic greeting Earthward.

The world's lush landscapes are heavy with the delightful promise of a brilliant future. Cosmically conscious humans are busy gathering Earth's richest treasures, a golden cache of spiritual growth and beauty. The truly wealthy store their discoveries, for rainy days lie just ahead. Sparkling like crystalline glass, the brilliant hues of the awakening are like beacons thrown into night skies. Like magnets, the light these humans emanate draws the restless to them. As the spiritually courageous are moved to share their mystical experiences, they challenge their soul-starved brothers and sisters to join them.

Share your abundant news! Do not hoard an excess of joy that may nurture others of less opportune experience.

Earth's rocky voice is calling her galactic kin from the far-distant stars to assist her. She grieves and sorrows over the abuse her human children heap upon her. Respect for Mother's health is sorely lacking. In sickness, do you not nourish and cherish your loved ones and they you as well? Do you not rub salves of gentleness upon their physical and emotional wounds? In like fashion, may you do also for Earth Mother—she who provides you with all the sustenance you require. If she loses her generosity and resiliency, life as you know it will cease to exist.

Those who persist in believing it is their right to take freely without giving, those whose activities destroy the planet's creatures, water, air, and land will eventually find themselves before a tribunal of the Spiritual Hierarchy. The abusive will find themselves hard put to explain to a holy being why it was they chose to participate in such activities.

Humans with the intention to practice the ways of spiritual integrity have begun to observe Earth's vibrancy from a different focus. A spiritually attuned person never approaches another life form with an attitude of ho-hum boredom or disinterest.

It is the privilege of this being of light, Palpae of Arcturus, to draft this segment of the galactic contract humans will be required to assimilate before they are granted status as fully activated members of the star councils. The Intergalactic Brotherhood's terms for adopting the citizens of Earth into the higher-resonating celestial ranks are set forth in the substrates of this manuscript. Humans are urgently advised that they must attend to the serious problems that confront them before they are invited to place their signatures upon any galactic contract. We warn you, celestial-based documents contain no clauses that may be broken.

Adonai this fine night.

The Guardians

Palpae

Earth is a savage world. Therefore, ethereal beings, commonly referred to as guardians or guides, steer their human charges over its dangerous terrain and in the harsh, untamed cityscapes that blot its lands. Guardians are beings of light who glide upon the glistening pathways of the spirit worlds, the refined vibrational realms that parallel the heavy resonations from which humans perceive life. They serve as protectors in moments of danger, as teachers, and as counselors.

To secure the attention of their (for the most part) nontelepathically inclined assignees, guardians use interdimensional gateways that blend Earth's environs with those of the ethereal. Commonly, guardians use symbolic techniques and visionary tools to communicate with their assignees through dreamtime and meditative imagery. However, many humans consciously tune their inner ears to the soft, telepathic voices of their guardians. It takes but a whisper to thought-link the spiritually discerning to their ethereal guides.

As you settle into the sleepy landscapes of dreamtime, invite your guides to accompany you. Trust that beings of light will appear to safely escort you through the drifting, transparent lands of the night worlds. But if you retire clutching fearful emotions to you, you issue an invitation to the shadowy figures of the night-mirror (nightmare) images.

When you cozy down as innocently as a newborn babe in its natal crib, expecting, as does any beloved child, to be serenely rocked, you will enter the dreamscapes in a much gentler fashion. Allow your lashes to fall gently upon your sleepy cheeks. Nestle yourself as if next to the warmest, most tender loving heart. Entrust your being to the beautiful light-entity that is, in truth, an extension of your Soul. Ask that the highest of the high attend you, those graceful beings who inhabit the brilliant lands of refined light. Safely protected, peacefully slumber.

Blessed are they who consciously converse with their guardians, for they know that these guardians are their dearest companions. When logical, intellect-entranced humans surrender themselves to the magical, mystical ways of their guardians, their hearts unfold like budding flowers. Whenever a human requests spiritual guidance and nurturing, it brings ecstatic joy to we who inhabitant the radiant worlds.

Guardians are always available to the spiritually evolving. They stand in constant readiness to assist the awakening, ready to help them move through the torments and turmoils that plague human creatures. They fluff away tendrils of karmic residue as if blowing them clean with the gentle breath of a summer's breeze.

Earth is in a state of transitional flux. In the turbulent years that lie ahead, Dark Lords will attempt to hitch an easy ride to the lower-vibrating worlds. Using their favorite pronged tool—fear—such shadowy beings effectively attach themselves to the unwary, like parasites upon host creatures. Monsters created from the energies of social turbulence, environmental decay, and human despair raise their ungainly arms, waiting to entrap the spiritually unconscious. Towering above the lands like giant, unruly serpents, Dark Lords permeate the lives of the cosmically ignorant, skillfully deflecting their attention from the radiant light emitted by the auras of the awakening.

Those of you who choose the high path need not fear the disruptive years, for you shine like lanterns in a stormy night. Eventually, the bitter days will pass you by. You who radiate unconditional Love sparkle brillant light and resemble the fire of newborn stars.

This message is transmitted from starbase Saturn, and yet Patricia detects no difference in the tonal quality of telepathic communiques originating from starships hovering closely above Earth and those originating from far-distant Saturn. Her telepathic experiences are teaching her that the space-time continuum holds no barriers to obstruct the flow of thought's natural pathways.

The Power of Music

PALPAE

Prior to developing techniques for maneuvering spacecraft outside your solar system, your scientists must understand that the operating mechanics of interstellar ships are built upon light, scent, and sound. They must recognize the properties of the grid system of spatial light strands and the manner in which the grid's intersecting points are positioned. They must study the delicacy of the strands' flower-scented hues and the subtle harmonics of their pitch. Thus, transforming mathematical computations into music is an initial step to commanding the intricacies of interstellar travel.

The knowledge that skillfully manipulated vibrations serve as our principal fuel source is not fundamental to human thinking. Indeed, it is unfortunate that the bulk of Earth's intelligentsia focus upon a mental-mechanical approach to science and that their dispositions are averse to the benefits of mystical wisdom.

Symphonies and concertos are nothing more than miniaturized adaptations of the power of sound when applied as numerical constants. Fifth- and sixth-dimensional beings view sound as a tangible substance. Sound is vibration. Vibration has the ability to swell, contract, ebb, and flow. Unlike waves, which are limited to rolling along in the ocean, vibration has the ability to thrust in all directions simultaneously.

Musical compositions are a natural form of telepathic communication. Music has the innate ability to transcend the barricades erected by divided beings who consistently misinterpret and misunderstand one another because of the limited resources of speech. Music, in all its forms, draws its listeners into a state of harmonic to-gather-ness. Musical notes have the capacity to create in unlimited fashion, from complex symphonic works to one-note repetitive chants. Music ebbs, flows, and pulses. It sets toes to tapping and tears to flowing. It is basic language, for its message is understood by everyone. In a real sense, music has already merged all Earth's people in commonality, for its melodies are universally comprehended and exclusive to none. One form of music may be more popular with a culture or age group than another; nevertheless, any misunderstanding that separates one from another is automatically bridged when a satisfying musical experience is shared.

Fading reverberations of harmonic songs played in ancient times continue to resonate around your planet. Their sounds still elevate and liberate the minds and emotions of vibrationally receptive people.

This essay includes only a few remarks regarding musical computations as energy. When scientists develop a clear understanding of the benefits of vibration as a "fuel" source and learn to use cosmic energy properly, they will free your astronauts from the terrifying prospect of traveling in space locked within the coffinlike housing of rocket-powered ships.

We encourage you to approach this manuscript with an open mind. Allow your intuitive eye to focus upon all references pertaining to hums, harmonics, hues, poppies, roses, and petals. Clues barely hidden within these paragraphs contain vital information for unlocking the secrets of interstellar travel. When understood, these keys will swiftly open the doors that prevent humans from attaining the stars. As the learned ones discover and embrace these data, they will be able to fling themselves into realms that only dreamers and mystics have imagined.

Humans, you will not happen upon the secrets of space flight by attempting to manipulate and submerge physical law with your domineering attitude of stubborn will. The space roads are accessed only by those who explore inwardly. You will not be allowed unlimited movement through space until your minds put to rest your fixation with metallic rocket ships and concentrate upon spiritual values, the works of Mozart, the subtle aromas of delicate flowers, the resonations of singing crystals, and the harmonics of Love-Light telepathy.

Make no mistake of the veracity of this chapter's song. To put our suggestions aside as renderings for the insane or scientifically inept will serve only to delay. With the hum of the planets and stars that smell sweetly of the space lotus, we spring from Arcturus to Saturn to Earth. As quickly as this thought is thought, thus it is accomplished.

Healing Earth and the Promise of the New Dawn

PALPAE

We encourage you to look for sleek starships barely hidden within the clouds. Hovering, secluded spacecraft hang close to Earth in these difficult times. The soft light of moonbeams illuminates our vessels. Glints from morning's first light bounce off our ships as sunshine reflects from glass windows. Stretch your heart-minds high into the skies. May the songs cloudships emanate inspire and guide you to seek God. May our silent voices bring a tranquil softness to your lives.

It would appear that you face a terrible fate. From your point of view, it seems possible that Earth Mother is losing her ability to sustain life. This brings dreadful images to the heart-minds of you who dare not dream a brighter future.

We are not unlike farmers who, when a harsh chill settles around the citrus trees, put out smudge pots to provide warmth. Always, our eyes keep watch upon the awakening as we anticipate their calls for spiritual sustenance. Our ships resonate hope as we work to satiate the ravenous appetites of the ripening. Day and night we pack our telepathic messages full of Love-Light's nurturing seeds. Each day our communiques are reborn while conscious-expanding humans sit upon couches, chairs, and rocks to record them. Diligently, these valiant beings struggle to clearly transcribe the ever-widening scope of our transmissions.

Humans are starved for the sweetmeats of hope and encouragement. Our purpose is to stave off their pains of spiritual hunger with an abundance of messages, for despair, frustration, and anger have become the prevalent thought forms.

Sand slips through the hourglass like quicksilver caught between the fingers of a clenched fist. No sooner do you close your eyes than you open them to greet the dawn of another day; shortly thereafter, night's curtain descends before the sun. Days scatter before you like tumbleweeds caught in a wind. In spite of the difficult times, hold trust and faith within your heart core. We reassure you: Hope's energy is securely tucked among the lines of this manuscript. Perceive all you do in a grand and enthusiastic manner. Do not forget that life's most delicious treasures are hiding within its simplest pleasures.

Planetary solvency remains. Earth is not yet bankrupt. There is still time to realign the disturbed contours of her ailing body. The Spiritual Hierarchy will not allow a violent disruption of her poles or an unstable wobble to cause her to wander off her assigned trajectory. Therefore, put to rest your anxious thoughts.

Celestial songs are sung by humans who gather into groups to share interests and purposes. Thousands have dedicated themselves to perform tasks of self, other, and Earth healing. It is our pleasure to observe humans who are committed to active participation in planetary healing. The passionate energy that these delightful men, women, and children radiate is invigorating to our essences as well. Whenever you join in Oneness to accomplish these things, you nurture your starry family in an energy-bonding fashion.

It would further please us if you would permit yourselves the luxury of letting go of all your sorrow-laden thoughts.

No matter the degree of anatomical complexity, all beings have an innate ability to focus upon That Which Radiates Love-Light. All things are endowed with some level of consciousness that is capable of concentrating upon magnificent Creator. It is inherent in all matter to seek Oneness with God. All form is genuinely receptive of radiant light emanating from Cental Sun's manifest energy. Infinitely vast, omnipotent, and omnipresent, Prime Power maintains perfect harmony throughout all creation.

Star councils (celestial management teams) comprise evolved Souls who are capable of sustaining and radiating light as substance. Contracts adopted by the councils are in accordance with the specifications of divinely inspired law. The beings who sit upon the councils maintain a strict policy of noninterference in humanity's affairs. Those who summon our guidance and seek spiritual illumination are invited to explore the documents contained in this and other multidimensional manuscripts. May our transmitted thoughts comfort you.

The emotions that have held humanity in Dark Lords' clutches will rapidly dissipate when society's greedy empires reach *crisis extremis.* As evolution is achieved, evil's festering sores will burst open like lanced boils. The grip Dark Lords have held will loosen, and they will find themselves escorted by the Spiritual Hierarchy to a planet vibrating at a lower rate than that of light-absorbing Earth.

Spiritually enlightened humans, the inhabitants of the new dawn world, will focus their life force upon adopting social principles based upon Divine Law. Joined as One in wholesome love, Earth's family of light will cheerfully clear away any remaining negative residue. Humans in the new dawn will bloom like hyacinths on a spring day. Their hearts will sing like birds greeting the morning sun. Cleansed and refreshed, the temperate winds of the new millennium will blow away the gloomy dankness of humanity's past. No longer will Earth's inhabitants hobble about as if they suffered from paralysis.

We strike this note as history's final hour approaches. Notice that we do not write a scenario of despair. Doom and gloom is only for those who prefer to follow the ways of Dark Lords. We caution you: Your choice of placement will be honored!

These thoughts are telepathed from the intergalactic starship *Marigold–City of Lights.* May the words of this essay settle around you in a warm, peaceful glow. We encourage you to wrap hope snugly around you and nestle down as if peace and tranquility held you in a warm, fuzzy blanket.

Blessed are you who live in accordance with the Law of One. You who understand know that humanity's difficulties are nothing more than a falsely contrived state of affairs arising from the manipulations of fear, and not that of Love-Light's greater intention.

Adonai.

Etheric DNA

Tashaba

DNA patterns basic to all planetary life are really third-dimensional projections of fourth-dimensional etherically aligned light. As a physical being, your primary tendency is to view yourself as something that can be seen, felt, and heard—a specialized assortment of bone, sinew, and the like. Nevertheless, the basic ingredient from which you are formed is essence of Soul. You are a spiritual being temporarily residing in a physical body maintained by an astral body, an emotional body, a causal body, a mental body, and a succession of continuously refining elements quite beyond our ability to adequately describe. DNA helix strands are the "glue" that attaches your physical body's cells to your light energies, or spiritual substance.

Your physical makeup is patterned upon a reflection of your spirit body; does it not stand to reason that your human body was fashioned upon structures of light? If you can view yourself in this manner, you will understand that alternative DNA is not a weird or mysterious happening but simply an initial step to prepare you to ascend into resonations of refined light.

The miraculous feat of providing a spiritual being with a material body is accomplished by "downloading" etheric DNA graphics into a sort of third-dimensional holographic printout. To aid in understanding the dynamics of this unique process, simply imagine an extraterrestrial humanoid figure shaped from light. When this image is clearly defined, surround your creation with a physical body. Behold! You have created a human being!

Many multidimensional telepaths have received the following information: In preparation for ascension, the human body will be provided with an additional twelve or thirteen DNA strands. The expanding number of strands marks the beginning phase of your physical merger into contours of light. The third strand will provide you with the Christ Essence—a cosmic indicator that, as Soul, will give you the ability to descend into matter at will and to re-ascend as spiritual light. This strand is a multidimensional ladder you will use to climb up and out of your physical body, enter and pass through your astral body, and exit into the realms where you will permanently integrate your light or spiritual body.

This information will help you better understand how starship personnel transfer genetic codes of endangered and extinct species onto the zoo ships. We do not beam up plant and animal cellular DNA strands. Our focus is to store their spiritual DNA in crystalline sleep cylinders. actively assist us by anchoring light onto the planetary grids whenever you participate in a sacred ceremony or meditation designed to heal Earth's plants and animals. For such a meditation, imagine a cord of brilliant light entering your crown chakra, passing through your spine, continuing down your legs, and going out the bottoms of your feet. Anchor this cord deep into Earth. Now, concentrate upon Earth, see her pollution-free, vibrant, and teeming with life. Your loving intention to heal Earth creates a powerful force that instantaneously pulses individual or group DNA essences up through your light-body and onto the zoo ships.

Do not concern yourselves with the fate of these wondrous beings. In time they will awaken and continue with their Soul work. They will be given a choice to recolonize upon another planet or to return to a restored Earth.

It is critical that you begin viewing yourselves as spiritual energy temporarily encased in physical bodies and to clearly acknowledge yourselves as powerful beings activated by thought. As such, you are bound not only by the physical laws of third-dimensional physics and biology but by higher-frequency Cosmic Law. As above, so below.

Tashaba's I Am presence is hopeful that this writing will help you gain knowledge on the protocol for processing physical DNA to etheric DNA.

On Time

PALPAE

Most humans are intellectually programmed to assess time in a linear fashion. Because of this, as Earth tunes herself to time's quickening energies, the neurons of the average brain are virtually incapable of adapting their synapse responses to time's rapid acceleration. Because of their propensity to focus upon the immediacy of their personal problems, humans are developing a growing sensation of being perpetually out of sync, which they find increasingly frustrating. They have little comprehension that Earth's time track has altered and that the flow of time alternately elongates and shortens.

When illusive time fragments filter into current time, you may find yourself startled by a sensation of déjà vu, a vague perception that you are witness to a past or perhaps a future event. The unexpected intensity of a déjà vu experience usually catches you off guard, an upsetting sensation to those who are uninitiated in time's mysteries. Although knowledge lies dimly remembered within your subconscious minds, clear perception of time's illusive ways is limited to those who have psychic sight.

Travel through time is unsettling to the unprepared, and they are apt to worry about their sanity. Those deeply concerned will often seek help from those adept in the complexities of the human psyche. Unfortunately, paranormal knowledge is not an area of expertise for Earth's "healers" of the mind. Few American- or European-trained physicians possess even a rudimentary understanding of time's ability to jump forward, backward, and side to side.

You may remember watching a movie that contained a scene whose characters struck you as startlingly familiar. Because of your cultural distrust of déjà vu, perhaps you attempted to satisfy your curiosity by explaining that whatever triggered the abrupt, perhaps intense, sensation was nothing more fanciful than something recalled from a book. Nevertheless, those experiences can be indicators of past or future Soul Memories erupting into present moment via a quirk in spatial time.

When you were born, you came into the world with your Soul Memories more or less intact. This pleasant state was briefly held within your newborn mind while the somnolence of Earth life settled into your consciousness. As you laid aside your precious Memories, it was as if you had taken a magnificent container and placed it in storage. When life ends and you wind your way through death's transitional stages, you will once again awaken in your spirit body and remember to recover your Soul's precious documents. You will take that dusty box, wipe it clean, unpack it, and place before you for meticulous examination all the things that make up the greater you.

Few retain psychic sight throughout life; fewer still have the ability to peek around time's corners. As magnified Earth is transported into the rapturous melodies of the new dawn age, awakening humans will be freed from the bondage of psychic blindness. Then, like the coming together of a gigantic puzzle, a complete picture of their Souls' eternal perfection will be clearly comprehended.

Adonai.

Great the Day That Sees Starships

PALPAE

Great the day that sees starships. Great the morn when we, the citizens of many suns, cascade from the skies to greet our human brethren face-to-face. Surely, on that glorious day the entire cosmos will resound with the tones of ecstatic rejoicing.

Capture our vision. Allow yourself to linger upon the magnificent moment when you regain the ability to travel to the stars. Do not turn away in fear of that day, for surely it is to come. The wonder you so often feel when gazing upon the face of nature will seem nothing more than a drop of rainwater in comparison to the vastness of your ancient Soul's playground, the depths of the majestic stars.

Quiet yourself. Fold inward as do evening flowers. In silent meditation reach into the calm, undisturbed stillness that is representative of your connection to the Divine. Move into a state of receptive clarity and allow an image of iridescent beings to float before your inner eye. As our forms serenely waver and fade, go deep into the light, into the sweet serenity that is indicative of your higher Self's connection to Creative Source. In this heightened state of meditation, you will begin to experience the reality of the subjective, etheric planes as easily as you experience the reality of the objective, physical plane.

Scan the shapes of clouds in the sky. As you awaken to our presence, flash a mental note to our starships whenever you detect a hint of their presence within clouds' fluffy contours. At such times, you grant us permission to convey nurturing thoughts of Love and warmth to you. As you come to a greater awareness of our mission, on a personal level you will begin to master the overwhelming emotions and events that threaten your peace and destabilize your equilibrium. As you acknowledge starships in residence Earthside and understand our intentions, you will be far ahead of humans who do not even vaguely question our motives.

Inevitably, your attention will be drawn away from clouds shaped like starships. By necessity, you must attend to the busy-ness that rightfully occupies the greater portion of your time. However, it takes only a slight effort to casually monitor the skies, simple use of moments well spent for those wishing to stretch their psychic muscles. A perceptive mind is a well-trained mind. If you desire to train your mind to become as supple and as graceful as an athlete's body, you must learn to constantly flex the substance of your thoughts. If you wish to activate the full potential of your brain, you must become mentally disciplined. As you begin to fine-tune psychically, your intellect will assure itself that extrastellar beings of light are in Earth residence. Then you will begin to walk life's roadways with increased tenderness and vigilant affection.

As you will it, we are yours, but surely not as conquerors and overlords come to enslave you. Indeed not! We are entities formed of Love-Light essence. Deeply we yearn to reestablish our ancient relationship with our Earth-based family.

Humans, the gravity of your situation requires your immediate attention and a refocus of your priorities. The parameters of human society swiftly shrink as the worldwide computer network facilitates everyone to instantaneously gather and store information. Clearly, you are all sitting in each others' backyards.

We challenge you to undertake a vigorous remolding of your rigidly structured and dogmatic religious, political, military, and economic institutions. Changes of such magnitude must originate in the hearts and intentions of humans of high integrity.

Universal Law does not permit us to sidestep your free will or to force radical revolution upon you. Rightfully, you would only resent and resist us. Because our position is one of noninterference in your internal affairs, we serve in an advisory capacity. It is not our place to thrust terms and conditions of Prime Law upon a people who hold no patience with outside interference.

Nevertheless, the number of those who fervently and conscientiously attempt to revamp the texture of their lives escalates. Humans who structure their values upon spiritual law are raising Earth's vibrations toward critical mass, maximum torque energy. Eventually, predictions the prophets recorded will come to pass and future time will lodge in present time.

These essays are carefully prepared and transmitted through the dialect tones peculiar to the nature of this Earth scribe. Our intent is to clearly state our position in such a way that the meaning of the messages is easily assimilated. Because you adorned your home with this manuscript, you will discover that you, too, are invited to communicate with beings of light who freely navigate the spatial grids.

As an Arcturian ambassador of the Intergalactic Brotherhood of Light, it is my honor to help humans prepare for contact with fifth- and sixth-dimensional extraterrestrials. Conditions must be met before you are invited to peacefully resonate with the diverse, harmonious beings who make up the greater galactic community. We anticipate you will take careful note of our stipulations as outlined within this manuscript.

Adonai.

Seeking Purpose

Palpae

We have come from the stars for the purpose of facilitating and coordinating evolutionary Earth changes. As one of numerous galactic ambassadors in residence within this solar system, it is my pleasure to participate in these matters in accordance with my Soul's objectives. Services provided to my human family are a privilege of my Soul contract with Source Creator and are joyfully performed by this being of light.

All clauses and subclauses for an entity's life work, or purpose, are recorded in agreement with Soul's contract with the Spiritual Hierarchy. All beings have a driving desire to activate Soul purpose. In humans, the mechanics that activate it are triggered through preset, encoded signals from the higher Self, transmitted as pulses of passionate desire through the heart-mind, relayed to the brain-mind, and then sent through the nervous system to stimulate behavior response. The ability to appropriately process one's purpose energy is predicated upon the individual's vibrational level and degree of spiritual refinement.

When spirit is born into third-dimensional physical form, it enters life with its purpose agenda close at hand. Purpose agenda resembles a geologic contour map in that the peaks and valleys of life's mission are meticulously outlined and embedded in the rich soil of the subconscious mind.

Your higher Self is a wise and powerful invisible force, the ruler behind your subconscious mind. It dispenses the abundant diversities of purpose through energy impulses that urge you to concentrate upon your life mission. Your higher Self is your direct link to Prime Power. It is a substation, a power plant that receives impulse relays from Divine Source generator and directs their harmonious energies to you. Being of physical form, you are like a lamp plugged into an electric outlet. To successfully access and shine energies of Divine Purpose into the world, you must consciously plug your subconscious conduits into higher Self.

You are connected to Soul energy through fibrous strands of light. If you have experienced an out-of-body state, you may have been more or less cognizant of a silvery-gold cord trailing behind you. Energies sent to you from your higher Self are directed through this cord in much the same way wire conduits supply power to electric appliances. You are joined to your Soul through ropey tendrils of light like a fetus is attached to its mother by its umbilical cord.

When you choose to switch off your spiritual light, that is, whenever you turn attention away from Prime Energy, the functions of your purpose become virtually inoperative. As lamplight is immediately available when its switch is turned on, your Soul's quiescent energy is instantaneously accessible to you when you feel at One. The marvelous feat of energizing purpose cannot be achieved without tapping into Prime Energy any more than a lamp can shine by itself without electrical stimulation.

Most humans do not recognize their right or ability to tap into the cosmic energy pool. Dysfunctional feelings of emotional separation from Source Energy, from God, is what turns off their power switches. In many, purpose energy flickers so low that it barely idles.

Always an act of integrated personal will, prayerful meditation is essential to retrieve and assimulate Soul energy. You who are spiritually activated are light solid. You resemble stout lighthouses on stormy nights. Valiant beings, you labor to push aside the heavy waves of malevolent fear and negativity that threaten to engulf the sleeping people of Earth.

The Human Caretakers

PALPAE

Angellike entities, beings of light who keep the space webs sleek and shining, are patiently retuning the cellular membranes of Love-Light seeking humans to resonate at the same frequency as Earth's refining vibrations. This heavenly chorus surges brilliant light whenever awakening humans endeavor to connect themselves to their higher Selves' melodic voices.

This brief message is meant to inform you that angel-like beings are the designated guardians of the ethereal realms. In similar manner, you are the cosmically designated caretakers of the physical world.

But we notice you have been rather shoddy in fulfilling your caretaker responsibilities. The destructive relationship you hold with Earth Mother is graphically evident, and your inability to maintain a harmonious relationship with the animal, plant, and mineral realms accurately portrays the truth of this statement. In particular, you exhibit an extreme lack of intention to interact with nature in a peaceful manner. Your leaders repeatedly fail to cleanse pollutants from the air and water, to protect the forests, and to nurture animal and plant habitats. Such an unenlightened display of environmental disinterest is indicative of an unsolicitous approach to caring for nature's magnificence.

Despair swiftly overcomes those who fully assimilate the gravity of this teaching. The amount of negative energy prevalent in your societies not only affects the relationships you have with one another (your primary focus of interest) but also touches the citizens of other star systems. Like it or not, human family, you are viewed by members of the greater galactic community as cosmically immature. Surely it is not too difficult to comprehend that Earth's deteriorating, poisonous state is duplicated in human society as deleterious bickering among your so-called nations.

It would behoove you to diligently clean house as if long-awaited visitors were soon expected and cobwebs hung about the mantels of your once-stately home. We of the stars are your long-expected but seldom-recognized guests. Unfortunately, starships arrived much sooner than you anticipated. Surely you were caught off-guard with your collective britches down. We caught you at a time when the odors of your garbage raise fumes into the naturally sweet-smelling air.

Polish up your sumptuous home! Make her beds with freshly laundered linens. Do so, so that you can stand proudly before the galactic elders on the day starship inhabitants ring your collective doorbell. In your heart of hearts, come to know that as you are presented to the magnificent beings of light, you are their equals. On that day, your representatives to the star councils will walk into the galactic chambers with their faces scrubbed and with no apologies necessary.

Humans, you face a difficult period in the years that loom immediately ahead, for time is rapidly accelerating. As the days flee swiftly down the corridors of time, your perceptual bearings will twist and turn as you move in new and untried directions. As Earth Mother struggles to don the garments of a light, more mature planet, humans wishing to continue life's vibrancy of necessity must learn to blend their physical impulses with those of Earth's quickened tempo. From a human point of view, energy patterns delineating Earth's transitional status are so subtle that they are difficult to detect. Nevertheless, their accumulated results will eventually become too dramatic not to notice, even to the most persistent spiritual sleeper. As Earth molds herself to fit into evolution's gown, she alters the passage of time. Though their clocks argue otherwise, humans' internal timekeeping mechanisms will be quite aware that the length of an hour dwindles.

Tumultuous years stretch ahead, years when the mental, emotional, and auric bodies of humans who have blocked the Memories behind a wall of intellectual amnesia will be pricked into awakening by the vibrations of their sorrow-laden hearts. Commit yourselves to taking active parts in smoothing and softening the heavy energies that circle Earth, for without the help of dedicated humans a period of chaos, in the form of natural and human-triggered disasters, will ensue during the century's dying years and into the early years of the twenty-first century. We urge you to press eagerly and urgently ahead on your quest to attain at-One-ment with God. Seek naught else but to appease your Soul's insatiable appetite.

Those who maintain high spiritual integrity will digest our comments, will clearly understand them, and will fully commit to light-body integration. We are aware of the courage and effort it takes for you to overcome deeply ingrained negative tendencies; however, as you establish a responsible approach to life, you will begin to surmount the disharmonious energies that hold you captive in physical form. Be aware that you must become spiritually active before you can master ascension into the light realms.

The Wonders of the Universe

The Arcturians

To be cozy in front of a fire with its dancing flames keeping winter at bay, to run free with body exposed and hair flying, to prance through the brilliant rays of summer's blessed warmth are a few things that truly nurture your human hearts. The moments when the adult you gives permission to your childlike self to engage in spontaneous play are your most precious times; your senses burst with the miracle of ecstasy experienced and the joy of life's simple wonders.

As you busily attend to your daily tasks, you are observed by beings of light who ride Earth's skies in cloud-cloaked starships. There are many written accounts of the watchers. Startling tales of UFOs and extraterrestrial visitations lay gathering dust in government archives. Fearing to meet the wonders of the universes head on, most humans, whenever they do think upon these mysteries, tend to envision us as oddly formed creatures intent on invasion. For the most part, access to our human family has been limited to accounts of UFOs in the tabloids, which provoke laughter, and in top secret government files. The topic of alien visitation receives little serious attention, and skeptics see no credibility in scattered reports that talk of military aircraft skirmishing with flying silver-disks.

Periodically, humans take time to ponder upon the reality of extraterrestrial visitation; however, when the tales become too weird, they become fearful of the motivations of the little green men and the creepy-crawly monsters, and their attention quickly reverts to subjects more satisfying. Few have any tolerance with governments or scientists spending time or money to investigate any form of bizarre paranormal phenomena. Nevertheless, the entire spectrum of human history and literature contains accounts of such extraworld activities.

Fear-ridden extraterrestrial encounters are limited to darkly negative beings and certainly are not the intention of fifth- and sixth-dimensional beings of light in service to Universal Law. Intergalactic Brotherhood of Light starships seek out humanity with Love-Light energies. Unsophisticated as you are in regard to universal cosmology, you are, nevertheless, members of the greater galactic family. You are our comrades in space and time. We do not wish to titillate your imaginations or to cause you fear. Our purpose is to help you transform spiritually and achieve ascension into bodies of light. It saddens our nature that those who focus upon the enticements of negative, addictive behavior will learn little from our words.

While we wait your return, we resume our place in the hollow recesses where you place everything you choose to ignore, for we know that after centuries of inordinate delay, the evolving are close to achieving status in the star councils. Eventually, it will be fashionable for you to discuss how amazed you are that you perpetuated such resistance for such a long time.

Popularity is vitally important to the average person. Many seek love and approval from others in order to fashion a worthy opinion of themselves. Is this not so? Though it may appear that we tend to greatly chide you, we do not do so from a position of judgment or of false superiority. It is simply that our ability to perceive consequences and ramifications of self-destructive behavior is much clearer than yours. Though we are privy to knowledge of humanity's volatile tendencies, it diminishes not one iota the degree of love we bear for you. Note that our transmissions always speak of the essential beauty of human nature.

The situation Earthside is gravely serious. While your leaders, those who carry the burden of responsibility for society's health, are struggling to hold onto their slipping reins of pseudopower, the broken hearts of the common people ache to get on with the grooming. Planetary healing and sound ecological practices are not popular with persons interested in maintaining status quo, yet in every sector of Earth's damaged crust the very ground beneath their feet festers with turbulent, feverish boils ready to erupt.

Every being, no matter its planet or sun of origin, who resides aboard the chariots of the Intergalactic Brotherhood does so by agreeing to harmonize in accordance with the tenets of Universal Prime Law—integrated Love-Light Intelligence. As you achieve greater awareness of the vastness of your galactic family, you will cheerfully begin to dismantle your massive, overwhelmingly complex laws. You will place their residue into barges and set them quietly adrift down the misty corridors of a best-forgotten past.

All beings are bonded to the Law of One by their Souls' purpose and willing service to Divine Principle. The radiant energy of the Law of One draws all beings to the warm hearth of Celestial Home, omnipotent, omnipresent, omniscient rapture, the core of the Central Sun, from whence the heartbeat of this universe issues God's Divine Energy.

It is our pleasure to outline, as simply as possible, terms of the galactic contract that is prepared and awaiting the signature of evolved humanity.

Discernment When Dealing with Negative Extraterrestrials

Palpae

It is critical for you to understand that dark, abusive extraterrestrials do exist, beings with advanced technology who are interested in controlling human society and dabbling in multispecies genetic manipulation. These beings are well known in UFO circles and in the new age community; they are referred to as Grays, men in black, and so on. Though various kinds of extraterrestrial visitors are known to some humans (see "Suggested Books and Movies"), we will refer to all negative-minded extraterrestrials as Grays. (Dark Lords can be in human as well as extraterrestrial forms.)

Grays are beings originating from several star systems such as Orion and Zeta Reticulum. They have deliberately separated themselves from the greater galactic community and the restrictions of Universal Law so they may be free to practice their diabolical ways upon sleeping humans.

Grays are fascinated with the games humans play, for they, too, find pleasure in indulging themselves with fear's intrusive ways.

A close encounter with a Gray certainly provokes terror, yet a confrontation with these godless entities is sure to widen one's viewpoint as to the nature of reality. Albeit having a rude awakening, a Gray's victim is apt to be jolted into turning tail and running home to God.

The lower vibrational dominions, which include the third-dimensional and lower fourth-dimensional astral plane octaves, are replete with negative beings enraptured with Dark Lords. Extraterrestrials who abduct humans are among Dark Lords and their followers.

It will help you understand the abducting aliens' point of view by considering the following: Most humans believe animals should be used as food fodder, as zoo captives, and as subjects for biological and genetic experiments, habitat relocation and demolition, and scientific investigation such as drug therapy and surgical technique exploration. Most humans look upon animals as having little import other than to serve the will of their human masters. Well, abducting extraterrestrials view humans in much the same way. To them you are a lesser species; in fact, they hold you lower than animals because of your compulsion to soil and destroy the environment of your home planet. No other animal degrades its living quarters in such a fashion.

Conversely, beings of light view all life forms as sacred, as essences of Divine Principle in manifestation. Vibratory placement does not mean one is better or lesser than another. A child attending kindergarten is not looked upon as being of less worth than a college graduate, only at a different stage in formation and development. The things you teach your beautiful children—knowledge of things, places, events, people, and language—are wasted if the foundations of these children and the subjects you teach are not rooted in the Law of Cosmic Intelligence.

To ensure your safety, it behooves you to maintain clearly delineated boundaries around your energy (auric) field. (See "Psychic protection" in the Glossary.) Do not fool yourself into believing that all extraterrestrials are dedicated to serving Omnipotent Light. Not all extraterrestrial energies visiting Earth are interested in spiritual evolution. The motives of some are self-serving and their methods are harshly destructive.

Universal Imperative Law operates on a freewill frequency. As such, the philosophy of light-serving extraterrestrials is structured upon the precepts of self-responsibility, as the Law of Free Endeavor clearly implies. In compliance with this law, the Oneness that makes up the star councils maintains a firm policy of noninterference in the affairs of negative-serving entities. Nevertheless, when extremely destructive elements critical to Earth's overall stability develop, we do step in and make a few energy adjustments here and there. Situations warranting our interference include imminent danger to the planetary body as a whole, launching of full-scale nuclear war, and an attempt by Dark Lords to take complete control of human society.

Dark Lords are both clever and controlling. In these closing years of human history, as humans understand it, Dark Lords are primarily occupied in tracking swings in human energy patterns. Earth is tenuously held as she slides inevitably to heightened critical mass and the transdimensional energy window that awaits her.

Information on alien abductions is rampant in modern times, for humans delight in frightening themselves more than they delight in uplifting themselves. This extremely unfortunate circumstance doubles star council efforts to incorporate intense refined light in this place of shifting darkness.

Are abducting aliens wrestling away your innocence? Innocence to and from what? No unsavory being can disconnect your Soul's innocent conduits to Divine Truth. If you view these unhealthy entities with compassionate understanding, you will know that like many humans, they, too, are about to miss an opportunity to upgrade their Souls' resonate status when Earth bursts higher upon the galactic planes. Extraterrestrials who represent the forces of darkness are very much like cold-hearted humans who struggle in vain to regain the loss of their love's once-innocent blush.

Communicating with Extraterrestrials, and Mutual Evolution

PALPAE

Manitu, you summon the name Palpae. Within the recesses of your visually active mind floats an image of this being of light. I venture forth from my distant home star to explore the feasibility of establishing nonverbal communication between spiritually evolving humans and the diverse beings who make up the star councils. Interdimensional telepaths who record our thought-to-thought exchanges greatly assist our efforts. Human channels who document their conversations with us and then share them are erecting a rainbow-hued superstructure made of floating tendrils of harmonic light. This structure will eventually span the mysterious gulf that separates humans from their extrastellar family.

Unrelenting desire to serve Soul purpose, no matter how subtle or insignificant activities may seem from your limited viewpoints, greatly facilitates our work in quickening and refining Earth's vibrations. Challenge yourselves to intuitively expand your concepts of the universe beyond physical reality and to delve further into the universe as spiritual reality. As you do so, it will serve to your advancement beyond anything you have ever imagined.

As we observe the accelerated rate of your awareness, we become ecstatic. It supplements our natural joy to see the escalating numbers of committed, dedicated, deeply spiritual light-integrating humans. You would be amazed to know how long we have hungered for your return to the stars!

You who concentrate upon receiving information directly from your guides are rapidly concluding that telepathic intercourse with fifth- and sixth-dimensional extraterrestrials gives you a substantial boost in your efforts to achieve God-Oneness, or ascension. It may surprise you to know that as you move up the ladder of spiritual awareness, your guides also receive a boost of energy at a magnitude third-dimensional instruments are incapable of measuring.

Previous methods used by the Intergalactic Brotherhood to awaken humans from self-induced cosmic coma have failed dismally. Opportunities given humans to reestablish peaceful resonations with their intergalactic family have been abruptly and forcefully rejected by power-hungry Dark Lords. However, with the influx of light-enhancing energies flowing onto Earth, humans are beginning to stir from their fitful torpor and it is becoming easier for beings of light to assist them.

On a more uplifting note, preparations for announcing full-scale contact between humans and beings of light take on an air of expectancy. By way of appeasing your impatience and any remaining anxieties, remember this: There has never been, nor could there be, any real separation between us. Only a flimsy illusionary barricade—a band of vibrating light—divides the fifth and sixth dimension from that of the third and fourth. The only thing that stands between you and us is an artificial spatial time facade—and your pervasive fear of the unknown. Moving starships from one vibrational density to another is similar to practicing scales upon a piano.

As a galactic ambassador, it is my pleasure to pave the fine highway of peace, to lovingly wipe away any remaining fearful images that blot your heart-minds from accepting the fact that soon you will be interacting consciously with beings of stellar light. Set aside your fatalistic notions about the future, for the day is coming when the Cosmic Broadcasting Network will broadcast the truth of Love-Light for all the world to hear. Then we will welcome one another in a discovery of mutual ecstasy.

All beings are about evolving to vibrational God status. That is our mutual dream, our mutual purpose. Nothing less is even conceivable. Currently, the multidimensional universe that is our mutual home is undergoing intense resonation adjustments. Powerful energies spiraling forth from Central Sun are rapidly elevating and refining the universe's vibrational pitch. In divine holy Oneness, we have all hitched a ride upon the sublime cosmic stallion that is inexorably pulling us all closer to Celestial Home.

The humming notes of this song fade. They sing of the magnificent fleet from the stars. From the stars, human family, from the stars.

Aummmmmmmmmm, Amen. Amen.

Joy! Behold Its Wonders

PALPAE

Mountains stream across the horizon where they stretch to meet the sky, a sky bustling with clouds that contain beings of light who hail from far-distant stars. We come from places you can barely imagine, though our home suns are easy to see.

Spin away your fears and rest contentedly in the arms of a glorious future. You are rapidly advancing to a higher state of cosmic maturity. You are to become one people, united, free of war. Bonded together in solemn recognition that all things are One, you will find yourselves in constant communion with Supreme Divine Creator. Those who surrender their pompish attitudes, childish displays, and grim sullenness for more joyful attitudes will find themselves accompanying Earth as she receives her holy banner, the royal insignia of a light-vibrating planet.

Lay aside your fears, for they are all imaginary. As you read the essays of this manuscript (and others like it), we anticipate you will encounter enough information to lay all remaining anxiety to rest.

Fear is the only thing that holds you stagnant in a lonely past. Love is the key that will release you to walk freely along the hallways of our massive starships. As your awakening minds open, the illusion of fear will dissipate as if driven away on the breath of a fresh spring breeze. As the last vestiges of fear evaporate, you will bond together as One people. Joyfully, you will establish upon Earth a serenely beatific society, a state of the cosmically mature. Then it will become a common occurrence to see you wandering our hallways, and many fine feasts will be held in your honor.

Fortunes will be made on the day you rejoin your star family, not for gathering material bounty, but for harvesting your Souls' great treasures. You will call out in joyful thanksgiving as you realize you have achieved ascension into your light-bodies. Voices united, you will cry out God's true name. To the spiritually blind, deaf, and empty it will appear that many voices reverberating as One will call out the names of many gods, but throats that speak in Oneness always resonate God's true identity.

As you come to realize the holy principle that Prime Creator ultimately draws all beings back to Central Sun, you will understand that there has never been any separation among you, us, and God, not ever or forever. Oneness with the greater cosmos comes on the day you put to rest the tragedy of dualism's unpleasant memories.

Silently, those who awaken link their minds with beings who hold the reins of silver-hued chariots from the stars. As they acknowledge the truth of our presence, they know there is nothing to fear, that we are as real as the grasses and bushes that grow around their homes.

Periodically, you may catch a brief glimpse of a metallic saucer skipping around the sky, though it is not our preference to adjust our light vibrations for the purpose of entering third-dimensional space. Our fifth- and sixth-dimensional starships are more adaptable to bonding their resonating hums into subtle cloud shapes. Little energy is expended when we berth our starships in the fluffy shapes that inhabit Earth's skies.

We delight in bunching together in the form of clouds. We dance and turn and stretch into long, straggly wisps before we disappear from human view. It is most pleasant to assemble and disassemble and to match the singing crystals that propel our starships with the brilliant vibrations of sun-drenched clouds. The clouds' pristine qualities are always honored; starships touch not their integrity with harmful trace residue. Welcoming our presence, the clouds continue to ply their way between sun and Earth undisturbed as they fulfill their function of cooling and dispersing life-giving droplets upon parched and thirsty lands. It is as wonderful as your hearts dare hope: The presence of cloud-shaped starships herald the promise of a glorious future, the dawning of a bright new day.

Glory is at hand!

Your evolution to light will be delayed if you worship material objects as if they were personal possessions. For example, if you were to approach gold with a higher regard, as if it were a healing emollient, its beauty would comfort and nurture your wounded hearts. Coveting gold for the sake of coveting gold is never generated by the pure in intention, those who joyfully share their abundance for the sheer ecstasy sharing brings them. If all the stacks of hoarded gold were equally divided, it would vastly enrich all of you. Humans will never experience the reality of true ecstasy until one person's gold becomes everyone's gold.

Humans cower in fear of a one world order, for they dread losing their will to the exploitations of capitalism, communism, socialism, Platonism, or other form of political, religious, military, economic, or scientific demagoguery. They do not understand that Oneness heralds the promise of a golden future, that the squalors of dogmatic thought foster the pain of duality. They suffer from the painful illusion that they are exempt from practicing Universal Law.

Rigorously, you bottle up your greatest desires. Your logic-loving intellects allow little room to explore the beautiful visions the mystics dream, and it greatly troubles you when you fear you cannot grasp the abundant substance of truth. But it is no longer necessary for you to wallow in a sea of sadness and lack of worth. Yank out and toss away that rotten old cork that keeps you clinging to the terrors of your past. Permit all that you truly are to flow magnificently free. May the suns of your days, the moons of your nights, and the outlines of starships barely hidden in clouds bring you the awareness that you are being saturated from space with beams of loving light.

Rich tones sung by celestial trumpets announce the return of the holiest of holies. May His Love-Light dwell gracefully in your hearts. There is no need to furrow your brows in somber despair. Your exquisite dreams are becoming fact!

Search inward continuously. It is essential, when receiving explicit instructions from your guides, to gravely consider and carry them out with careful attention to detail.

The terrors of humanity's war-provoking behavior is only a sullen attempt of one fearful people to smother the light energies of another. Learn to speak to one another from the vibrant beauty of your hearts as lovers do, not as warriors do. In all you think, in all you do, lead lives that emanate healing rays of compassionate Love. Creation is in need of beings who call others to be with them as One. Shout your intentions clearly. Refine your habits and thoughts so that the power behind your message is never warped.

Peace transcends sorrow.
Sorrow transcends pain.
Pain transcends fear.
    Fear accompanies only darkness—
        the absence of Divine Light.
    Dispel fear and you will attain the stars.

Seek the stars and soon you will discover eternal life's vibrant flame. Those who sink backward into the slumber of disinterest and fear will find their awakening delayed to yet another fine day.

I address my human family in the tones an ambassador uses when speaking to the venerable members of an ancient and greatly esteemed court. May my words poke their way through your mind's resistance and melt the core of your heart's understanding. May they settle into the place where your spiritual wings wait to expand, where your thoughts meld with beings of light who greet you from the stars.

Earth Mirrors Humans

PALPAE

Earth's matrix mirrors your anatomy. To understand this analogy, begin by considering Earth's crust being made up of skin, hair, moles, dimples, and scars. Sit quietly and reflect upon this imagery. Then, following your breath as it moves through your nose, lungs, and blood cells, slide deep into Earth's body until you touch her magnificent heart. Continuing to use your breath, draw her vibrant energy upward. Visualize the powerful energies that circulate from her heart toward her surface. Invite her awesome strength to embrace and permeate your entire being.

Contemplate your body as a perfect reflection of your magnificent Earth Mother. Acknowledge that the full extent of her charismatic visage is not upon the skin of her surface but deep within her core where her spirit, her real power, dwells.

To allow opportunities for growth to escape would be tantamount to ignoring diamonds shining from a path without a backward glance to consider their beauty. Most of you focus your primary attention upon worldly things—money, material goods, and an enduring infatuation to control other people's lives. Such activities must end before you are permanently received into the light realms. Earth's luxuriant bounty is designed to teach you that preference for satiating your material appetites before gratifying your Souls' enduring hunger for God is analogous to ingesting a diet of only sugar and salt with no consideration for the resultant chemical imbalance in your organs. You cannot expect to heal your broken hearts by a shallow investigation of the causes of your pain. You must allot a time for courageous and intimate explorations of its depths as well as a time for healing.

A good day to those who assimilate the essence of this teaching. Though its nuances may appear overly simplistic, they are not without their fine points.

The Road to Harmony

Palpae

Hark to the hum of the stars as they whirl through space. Liquid suns, molten with the fires of God's Ecstasy, pour radiant light upon Creation's eternal immensity.

It begins: the time when peace and harmony sprout from the fertile seeds of discord. Be aware that these years are grooming years. Earth Mother is about to turn the tables on you. She will wrap her tendrils around you like a clinging vine encircling a dying tree—not unlike the parasitic manner in which you have treated her. She is about to humble your domineering ways with a display of her awesome power. Particularly in the last hundred years, your industrial-based society has attempted to subdue her energies for its selfish and shortsighted purposes. But she will win the game after all. She will see to her health with scant comfort from the majority of her human children. Very pleasant years will follow her purging, quite pleasant indeed. And they will last a very long time.

Because nothing remains inert forever, evolved Earth citizens will be challenged to yet another initiation, another graduate-level examination. Before they become eligible to advance another grade in the cosmic schoolhouse, they will be required to complete preestablished curricula. In a manner similar to the criteria of your educational systems, a series of projects, tasks, and proficiency tests must be undertaken before they can move up the scale of vibratory refinement. But as wisdom and knowledge are gained, they can apply to their teachers, their higher Selves, who then recommend promotion to their superiors, the Spiritual Hierarchy.

The majority, however, are not the slightest bit aware of the particulars of, or are interested in, Soul promotion or even of their status within the cosmic placement system. In spite of this, their spiritual achievements (or lack of same) are automatically recorded in the Akashic Records. These chronicles of all Soul journeys are held in perpetual trust by members of the angelic realms.

Scattered on your planet are secret storage sites full of sacred information. These sites are in areas held sacred to indigenous people: mountain ranges, rock-formed temples, etheric and stone pyramids, and other wondrous places throughout the lands and under the seas. Humans who are about to complete their course requirements, those scheduled for ascension into their light-bodies, will soon receive codes to retrieve their records.

On Starships

PALPAE

You need search no further than your inner Self to discover beings of light whose far-distant planets circle serenely around their parent stars. Always we have been with you. In ancient times our light-pulsing ships traced rainbow-colored beacons before the stars. The Apache, the Arapaho, and the aborigine gazed contentedly at the beautiful configurations our starships drew. We were with you when Cro-Magnons traipsed on the chilly Russian steppes. We were with you when Egyptians began to erect mammoth pyramids. We were with you when Rome's brilliant moment breathed its final sigh. We were with you when bustling cities erupted on Britain's hills. We were with you when China's Great Wall captured her citizens behind its huge barricade. We were with you when massive stone temples sprouted out of the jungles of Peru and the Yucatan.

Our original contact is lost in the depths of antiquity. Patiently, we have observed the rise and fall of many human civilizations. We have tracked your progress along the long road that leads to planetary maturity.

Contemporary scientists focus gigantic telescopes upon the solar grids. Cautiously, in carefully phrased jargon, they explain that the dancing red, green, white, and blue pulsations heralding the presence of intergalactic ships are light-diffusing layers of atmospheric gas!

Listen carefully! Think clearly! Starships must abide by physical law. When we reduce our vibratory rate to occupy Earth space, our maneuvers are kept well within the laws of applied third-dimensional physics. What is easily accomplished with prisms of light is equally done with fog and clouds. Although we are quite capable of assuming the metallic appearance typical of your standard UFO sighting, it is not our preferred mode of travel. We much prefer to move through the quiescent harmonics of our fifth and sixth dimensions.

As the unknown becomes known, your perceptive viewpoints will begin to shift. Comprehend how Creation is truly fashioned.

Human Relationships

PALPAE

Those who travel through life clasped in the arms of their beloved Soulmates, who bond as one in joy-filled relationships, attain some of the highest levels of ecstasy known to physical beings. And those who live in abject poverty experience and express love's essence as capably as do those in their mansions.

A "chance" meeting occurs and two of you discover yourselves linked as one, as if you shared the same Soul. From the energies of beatific coupling your children are born and your family is established. Lavishly display your love for one another, for to love and to be loved sustains and vitalizes your lives. Even brief interludes of love barely shared bring respites of momentary peace to those who are tormented.

It is unfortunate that one of your favorite topics for titillating discussion is tumultuous self-other relationships.

The media are permeated with disastrous consequences of impropriety and abusive sexual energy that occur between lover and lover, friend and friend, brother and sister, parent and child. From generation to generation, the behavior of the adults dramatically influences the lives of the children.

When love's ecstatic energy is debased for the purpose of self-only orgasmic gratification, its golden promise is quickly reduced to tears that stream from the depths of sorrow-laden hearts. Indulgence in sexual intercourse without integrity eventually leads to a decline in self-worth. The damage done to your psyches through debasing life force energy is mirrored in the loss of nature's vitality through chemical pollutants and industrial waste. This is not a new story! Indeed, it has been a common practice throughout all human history.

Beings of light who are members of your interstellar family have prepared a pretty package for you and daintily wrapped and adorned it with shiny paper and an abundance of bright ribbons. A treasure chest full of delights and wondrous things awaits you.

We are aware that many of you distrust our arrival and are fearful we will dishonor our budding relationship by terrifying you with a Pandora's box of alien horrors. But for many, a growing awareness that they are bonding with members of the greater galactic community is evident in their awakening knowledge that humans are Soul connected to the stars.

Our telepathed messages rest upon your planet like a crown adorned with priceless jewels. As Earth ascends into the light realms, you will discover you have been encircled by Creation's most precious ornament, a garland of Divine Love. A comfortably fitting tiara, Divine Love's omnipresence is all-encompassing and embraces the entire spectrum of Earth's diverse beings.

Life and the Physical and Etheric Bodies

PALPAE

Developing a spiritual attitude (even if clumsily executed) provides a basis for evolving the mind and the emotions, expanding psychic abilities, and healing the physical body's cellular matrix. Ingesting heavy foods that settle like iron weights in the stomach does nothing to nurture the intuitive centers of the heart-mind, nor does a daily regimen of vigorous exercise do little more than keep the muscles firm and alertly poised, like a well-oiled machine. Those who strive to maintain a balanced, quality life allot time for stimulating exercise and playful activities, proper diet and appropriate rest, intellectual endeavors and emotional nourishment, and a reverent regard for the spiritual sustenance of their light-bodies.

Many are not comfortable by temperament, injury, dis-at-ease, or age to take an interest in energetic exercise programs to the extent as do the avidly athletic. Even completely paralyzed beings flex and bend their head muscles now and then to remind themselves that they are active participants in life's mysterious challenges.

Inevitably, the time arrives when the bodies of the most exuberantly healthy are beset with the frustration and pain of illness or accident. It is impossible to count the things that can disrupt the natural harmonics of a physical body and cause its fibers to pop and ping. In extreme circumstances, the terrifying face of mortal illness may suddenly announce its presence.

It may or may not surprise you that a signal sent into the ethers from a distressed mind is an invitation to all kinds of bacteria, viruses, and accident-accommodating gremlins to visit. It is common for waves of imbalanced energies to emanate from the mental, emotional, and physical bodies of spiritually undisciplined humans. Fearful mental and emotional energies produce a siren-like clamoring announcing that the host body is receptive to negative-realm astral intruders.

The physical torments which Earth beings endure are not known on the planets that sustain fifth- and sixth-dimensional beings in perpetual harmony. Understand that physical-dimension planets, like Earth, invite themselves to be used (in a manner of speaking) for a period of cosmic time. Planets occupying third-dimensional space know that their vibrational hums are best suited to provide opportunities for light-aspiring beings to complete their karma.

The notion that all things upon Earth are of Earth is not completely true. The Soul structures of many humans, animals, and plants were originally seeded from other star systems. Many animal and plant species that have undergone or are facing extinction will not opt to reincarnate upon Earth, although some will reestablish when human society is reinvigorated. We will escort many of them back to their home stars, such as Arcturus or the Pleiades, for which they silently yearn.

Come. Quiet your restless thoughts. Let loose your burdens. Relax and breathe slowly. With each successive breath settle comfortably into tranquility's peaceful place. Calm yourself. See yourself as a dawn sun peeking serenely above the horizon of a placid ocean. Hush! Become one with the quiescent you that dwells just below your turbulent thoughts. Surely a moment of meditative silence is more precious than a crown of ornate jewels. Relax and descend into the depths of your heart-mind's intuitive center. There is no need for anxiety as you retreat into the silent world of the inner Self, for your mind will remain aware of your physical body's vibrancy.

As you delve into the characteristics of your mind's conscious and subconscious states, it may appear as if you are viewing several separate categories of Self. Unaware people assume that their conscious activities are somehow disassociated from their subconscious (spirit) and superconscious (Soul) minds. Though it cannot be objectively proven that Spirit and Soul are experienced on the material plane, in reality the self-Self is One essence.

To illustrate: Although the lower portion of a boat is hidden below the surface and cannot be seen, the upper rtion is clearly visible. To image a boat resting partly .bove water and partly submerged is an apt analogy to describe the relationship your inner you—your higher, Soul Self—has with the more substantial-appearing outer you—your lower, physical self. It is only an illusion that your physical self and your Soul Self somehow reside in different places.

Though you are caught in the life-death recycling common to third-dimensional worlds, whenever you exit life's energies at the time of transition called death (*birth* is a more accurate term), your spirit body heaves a sigh as it frees itself from your physical body's oppressive weight. After your "between life" analysis is complete and you are ready for another go at Earth school, your higher consciousness shuts down and seals the doorways that open Soul's memory banks while your etheric body reintegrates into physical form. Your computerlike brain for the most part is denied access to the data your superconscious stores in its massive vaults.

As death overcomes your physical body, your spirit begins to process reality from a viewpoint of heightened clarity, far surpassing the limited abilities of all but the most advanced seers and spiritual masters. Soul awareness, however, is not necessarily granted to humans who failed to spiritually challenge themselves in life. People who focus all their attention upon lust, addictions, and other forms of abusive behavior send negative thought pulsating through their mental, emotional, and spiritual bodies. Caught in the tempting web of temporal desire that Dark Lords spin, humans who agree to drain themselves of light energy lose recall of the retrieval codes that access their precious Soul Memories.

Those who manipulate the lives of others (though outwardly appearing powerful and of pleasant demeanor), those who are consumed with a passion to serve Dark Lords' evil intentions, will surely perish from life as they know it. The spirit cells of those poor tormented beings are to be removed to an alternative planet where the elemental hum resonates at a denser pitch than that of evolving Earth. This world anxiously awaits her new inhabitants. It is a life untried and immature, a planet in a plane of existence outside the perceptual range of humans.

The Spiritual Hierarchy is busy recalibrating Earth's humming pitch to refined vibrational brilliancy, and the grid fibers of her light-body are being carefully realigned. Eventually, her rocky structures will become as fluffy as clouds. Be aware, as you prepare for ascension, that, like Earth, a quantum shift to light status can be accomplished only by retuning your vibrations to hum in accordance with higher-octave resonations. You are temporary boarders on Earth—noisy, often bothersome guests. As such, you are utterly dependent upon her generosity. If you choose to remain as an evolved Earth inhabitant, you must maintain your vibratory alignment at her adjusted level.

When you exit physical form you may discover yourself in an environment that seems startlingly familiar. Your naive expectation of emerging into a rosy, heavenly place full of glowing angels strumming ethereal harps is slightly askew. The majority of Souls on Earth assignment wade through lifetime after lifetime before their spirits evolve into the purified realms where physical death is unknown.

Soul's lives are like pearls that are precious beyond measure. Strung upon a common cord of Soul energy, they are quite spectacular. And remaining constantly vigilant of its many parts, the higher Self is the commonality that binds all your lives into One Soul life.

Competence in spiritual matters must be earned. Vibratory advancement is not automatically granted. It is important for you to carefully integrate this last piece of information. Most humans appear so bored by the prospect of entering heaven's pearly gates that they neglect to pledge themselves to personal evolution. Furthermore, they are unaware that dedicated commitment to light-body status is the primary manner in which third-dimensional beings serve That Which Calls Life Into Being.

We are of the opinion that we have presented you with a small tidbit or two upon which to chew. Essay after essay is designed to drop one golden nugget after another onto these pages, bits and pieces of wisdom wrapped so snugly in cloaks of familiarity that you may find yourself whispering, "Now see here, I know that!" These are mixtures of galactic homilies seeded through and through with gems of cosmic truth. However, you must discern for yourself how these little nuggets apply to your journey. Our objective is to help you clarify your life's deeper meaning and identify your Self's higher purpose. As you broaden your base of cosmic knowledge, we trust that the narrow margins in which you contain life's abundant resources will greatly expand.

You need not be alarmed if you are ignorant of religious philosophy, ritual, and customs. What is important is for you to integrate Love's energies in all you think, say, and do.

Adonai. This date's song stands complete; its last bar is hummed.

Encore

PALPAE

Cadaverous are the faces of humans who have lost hope. The future looms before them, and its vast borders are limited by their overwhelming sense of terror. Earth is full with men and women who have lost faith that Prime Creator will care for them, and in the process they have lost contact with life's purpose. For the most part, they allow themselves to be caught in the saga of life's ongoing dramas.

Many complex issues confront humanity, and a sense of overwhelming frustration may have been the impetus that, as a last resort, led you to open the pages of this manuscript. Yet the very act of seeking an alternative indicates that, at the very least, you somewhat recognize that a higher state of being does exist.

We suggest that in a meditative state you dive deep into the innermost recesses of your being until you begin to uncover hope's vibrant qualities. Activated, hope may be gathered as a tangible field of cosmic energy, a by-product that naturally arises when one *knows* one is of the Light, a Soul originating from the energies of the stars. Hope's melodies exude sweet harmonic sounds throughout awakening humans' physical bodies. Then its vibrancy spreads like filaments of light throughout their auric, emotional, and mental bodies.

As you stretch your minds and emotions to accommodate the fact that beings of light from the great star nation have surrounded Earth with a massive fleet of starships, you will undoubtedly find yourselves prompting families and friends to awaken to an expanded view of reality. With a wee bit of effort, you will assist others in moving to a place where they, too, can begin a conscious effort to dress their lightbodies in the finest of apparel. "Prepare yourselves" will be your call. "The journey Home is about to commence!"

Having forgotten that their Soul assignments are to serve Source Creator, humans resemble actors and actresses who have forgotten their lines. For the most part they numbly await some elusive, inspirational offstage prompter to tell them what it is they came to do. In this lifetime, all humans were granted an option to perform in one of only two dramas currently playing on Earth. The play on one stage defines the Soul's enlightenment on its long journey Home. The other play raises its curtains on a darkened stage, waiting to draw the unwary into the pits of a nether world. We advise you to decide carefully. There are serious ramifications awaiting those who make unwise decisions. It is up to all humans to precisely define their roles in each scene as the plot lines unfold.

The nuances of the opening stanzas of the greatest story ever told may have found you idling in the lobby. It will not serve your best interests to be caught napping for long, and it will certainly be impossible for you to be an observer indefinitely. Eventually, you will be called upon to mount the grand stage, and participate you shall!

Wishing to encourage self-activation in our human counterparts, we find it useful to use a performing arts analogy to help you understand that a dramatic worldwide saga is literally unfolding before your eyes. We also encourage you to understand that whatever brings pleasure and enhancement to your lives is equally nurturing to us. Whenever you express yourselves in a deeply spiritual manner, intense light pours from your heart-minds and moves through your auric fields in broad swaths of golden white brilliance. Concurrently, and with your higher Self's permission, the Love-Light energy you radiate attracts similar vibrational light frequencies that starships are constantly beaming Earthward.

The spirit bodies of humans who have committed themselves to fulfilling their Souls' greater purpose shine through the night skies like lasers, puncturing the last vestiges of darkness that once threatened to engulf Earth. Though your ego selves may succumb from time to time to despair and discouragement, calm yourselves with the benevolence of expanding consciousness. Continuously and courageously push yourselves forward. Fearlessly tackle life's challenges. Know within the deepest well of your innermost being that the journey Home is worth every ounce of effort it takes to get you there.

We urge you to become vitally alert to the times in which you live. An opportunity to play a significant role in humanity's finest hour is yours for the taking. Although not everyone is ready to tackle the demands of life purpose tasks, many, a very great many, are equal to them.

The rather narrow perspective from which you view reality is reminiscent of ants observing the sky from the depths of a hole. For the most part, you resemble amoebae swimming aimlessly on a microscopic slide, totally unaware of who or where you are and completely oblivious that you are being scrutinized. But in spite of your third-dimensional perceptual difficulties, many of you have determined that reality has a much broader definition than heretofore realized. Your growing intense spirituality has brought you to a point when you desire to rediscover your lost Self. Still, many unanswered questions continue to haunt you.

If you are one who studies the often-obscure, rather oddly worded documents that beings of light are releasing throughout the planet, you have already embraced a wider outlook and realization that the cosmos is much grander and far more expansive than anything you ever dared dream. Awakening ones, you may paint a more spacious landscape of your Soul's magnificent Home! The warm hearth of Central Sun is our mutual, ultimate destination!

It is unfortunate that throughout history humanity's brilliantly laid plans almost immediately turned to scrap and rubble, for the Law of Perpetual Abundance has been greatly warped by your willingness to allow Dark Lords to delude you and manipulate your energies. As your disturbing fluctuations are absorbed into Earth's delicate body, they are carefully monitored by starships. Potentially destructive waves of geologic imbalance are then quietly transmuted before Earth's tectonic plates become critically misaligned. When flows of disruptive energy float skyward, they are caught in starship crystalline beam nets, sweetly enhanced with harmonious light, and then safely released to drift onto the humming spatial grids.

Melodious, flower-scented, rainbow-hued cords of celestial light are pushing and pulling Earth toward an ever-expanding spatial window. Step by step, Earth advances closer to the moment when she will achieve her Soul's destiny. As time hushes, her magnificent body will slip into the canal of planetary rebirth, a portal that will propel her into the ecstatic hum of the fifth-octave light dimension.

Mimicking Earth's ascension into the Light, the entire universe is being calibrated by Prime Creator's tuning fork. All spatial universal segments are being refined and pruned of every trace of residual rawness. The solar winds shift. Masses of stars cry out from galaxy to galaxy as they challenge one another to gather as One in homage to Omnipotent Potential. As Source Light wills it, every inhabitant of the massive star colonies will be invited to drink from the crystalline goblet that holds the divine elixir of Universal Desire.

Higher astral beings breathlessly await Earth's deliverance into the realms of light. For as humans advance up the dimensional ladder, their astral counterparts do as well. All third- and fourth-dimensional entities best hold tight to their reins lest they fall off the bucking Earth steed in these heightened times. After Earth's magnificent vigor settles into a more rhythmic stride, those who remain will discover that malcontent beings have slipped from view and quite literally have been plunked into the gritty sands of an early-stage planet. Dark Lords and their followers—those who lack spiritual luster, those who willfully chose a state of prolonged graceless slumber—will be groomed and regroomed until a more auspicious moment in galactic time when they, too, will opt for spiritual maturation.

There is no time to squander! Deny yourself the luxury of indulging in self-pity. Unburden yourself of all obstacles that do not carry hope high within your breast. Embrace hope's optimum, transformative energy as an urgent priority. Hope tenderly held has the capacity to blow away all the cobwebs that linger within your mind. Dust hope off as if it were a long-ignored treasure chest of precious jewels. Do not allow a lackluster attitude or a spiritual listlessness to betray you into believing that you are headed toward a torn and tattered future.

Although Earth volunteered for her galactic assignment, she has piled on karmic debt. Like all beings caught in the heavy gravitational pull of the third dimension, she, too, is subject to the Law of Cause and Effect. But her debts are almost paid; soon she will be karmically free. Alas, humans, you as her principal caretakers have your own accounts to settle, and you are on borrowed time. You do not want to find yourselves abandoned at this late date for no other reason than you placed your bets on marked cards. In the cosmic game of "chance," a losing hand may always be exchanged for a winning one. Herein lies the trick. You all can easily win at this game. No losers are necessary.

The twentieth century is history's final full century. Now is when sorrow and war end. Love is already the victor. The battles that have kept you separated from one another will soon be laid to rest.

Palpae and Patricia join as one mind to create a solid structure of words bonded to paper. Our intention is to extend and enhance your awareness of the cosmos. We trust these writings will expand your knowledge of the nature of greater reality.

Adonai.

Interlude: Greetings from Tashaba

Dreams and Implants

Dreams are a psychic tool higher Self uses to break down the traditional, rational thought processes that block spiritual growth. Dreams are sleeping visions. Some are grandly pictorial; others are constructed from fragments of connected and disconnected thought. Many weave patterns of symbolic designs whose meanings are so obscure, so barely discernible that they defy analysis by the most astute dream reader.

In dreamtime, the subconscious (fourth-dimension, astral mind) and superconscious (Soul or higher Self) have access to the conscious mind for, among other things, answering questions and posing solutions to problems that elude the busy daytime mind. Disengaged from space-time physical restrictions, the astral body freely floats in mystical worlds that transcend the narrow confines of waking-state "reality," thus providing such answers and solutions.

The symbolic meaning of a dream may be obscure, as if its essence were covered by an impenetrable fog.

Ultimately, only the dreamer can uncover and interpret its significance. Often the message the dream carries weeps with frustration for its inability to wade through the barriers of resistance erected by the dream's third-dimensional counterpart, the brain.

Tucked securely into the innermost recesses of aware human's pituitary glands are multidimensional crystalline data chips implanted by fifth- and sixth-dimensional beings of light. These chips allow awakening ones to simultaneously receive and transmit thought from their guides and other multidimensional beings. The chips also provide each one with a personal solar library, a veritable storehouse of cosmic information that can be tapped into at will. Each one's Soul Memories are also recorded on the chips.

When we communicate with "channels," transmissions are changed to human language (in Patricia's case, English with a Western flare) within their minds. They are seldom conscious of the process. Channels tire easily when receiving, so "unused" portions of material are stored in the pituitary, similar to the way information is stored in a computer, for future retrieval. As channels increase in ability, we transmit increasingly complex information. This is observable with Patricia's writings, for her first volume is much simpler in content than are these pages.

If channels are incapable of integrating multidimensional information comfortably because of resistance based on rigid belief structures or the lack of basic scientific training, it is almost impossible for us to send intelligible data to them. They are apt to go into "glitch mode" if their minds and emotions are not at ease with material they cannot comprehend. The content of the transmission is also set by the emotional mood or vibrational state of the channel's conscious mind. Communiques originating in the minds of fifth- and sixth-dimensional beings are continuously tuned to the harmonics of the channel's emotional receptivity, life experiences, and perception of truth.

As you learn to decode telepathically received information into language, you will discover that you are walking, talking libraries of encyclopedic wealth. However, until you are spiritually activated, the bulk of this knowledge will, for the most part, remain inaccessible.

Thousands upon thousands of years ago (in some cases, millions of years ago) extrastellar Soul groups we refer to as wanderers or starseeds agreed to incarnate in a variety of physical forms for a certain time on Earth. As a subclause of their contract to serve Earth, they were not to know they each contained all Universal Mind computer bank (Akashic) records. Until recently, only the most advanced Souls were granted spiritual empowerment and permitted access to these records. As starseeds reach ascension status, however, and with permission of their higher Selves and the Spiritual Hierarchy, they will recover data the Intergalactic Brotherhood has implanted deep inside their brains.

Unfortunate above all other beings, humans fumble about in a ponderous manner, forever seeking easy formulae with which they hope to heal their fractured psyches.

Most do not realize that dreams and routine silent meditation are the quickest, cheapest, and most widely available remedy for that which plagues them. A mind serenely at rest is a potent pill, a therapeutic treatment to heal the physical, emotional, mental, and spiritual fatigue and aching discomfort that is chronic to the human condition.

Surely Tashaba sounds a fine note! It is discouraging to be told that you do not know what you think you know. Nevertheless, my intent is not to pacify you with sweet, gentle words. My purpose is to stimulate a passionate desire within you to move beyond the confines of Earth's third-dimensional boundaries. It is true: A fresh slant on a much-discussed, mutually interesting subject can often penetrate the most stubbornly resistant mind and provide it with a sudden flash of insight.

In telepathing this essay, it is my purpose to gather a small group of words that seem barely to begin a thought before they end. I will offer you little comfort of additional insight, for all great journeys are initiated by taking one golden step. It is the design of this communique on dreams and cosmic data implants to trigger your further interest, to inspire you to proceed with active exploration for what is truly wondrous: the multidimensional world that resides within your inner being.

Tashaba is my vibrational hum. My "name" represents an I Am energy that resonates in accord with Earth's animal kingdom. Feline in essence, my being's greater purpose is to encapsulate and protect the precious DNA patterns of Earth's endangered and extinct plants and animals. I, and others like me, are caretakers of starship crystalline vaults, where Earth's most priceless treasures are carefully stored for future retrieval.

Tashaba is pleased to briefly enter this manuscript's pages. Originally it was not planned for my presence to participate at this stage of the writings. However, it is my honor to be in attendance at Manitu's special invitation. Surely we would not deny her such a small favor.

Come hither and allow your minds to greet Tashaba. My form resembles those of the great cats of Earth; as such I stalk and prowl the wide corridors of fifth- and sixth-dimensional starships. My form is sleek and graceful, and I have a most loving disposition, yes, most loving. I desire you to know this. To comprehend and appreciate Tashaba's nature will provide you with yet another view of an expanded reality.

Human Difficulties and Mother Earth

Awakening starseeds are almost overwhelmed in these accelerated times as they whirl from one passionate mood to another. Sorrow is so deeply embedded within the cores of their slumbering hearts that they often feel as though the vibrant rays of the morning sun reflect nothing more than yesterday's pain. Such pain can be so pervasive at times that their only escape is interludes of dreamless sleep. Unattended, their pain descends into despair. Unattended, their despair becomes as persistent as a hungry cougar stalking its prey, unrelenting and ever present.

To transmute the agony of sorrow that haunts you, we suggest a thorough study of the multidimensionally telepathed books, articles, and films that are ever increasing. The discriminating will soon discover that beings who represent Love-Light have the greatest compassion and understanding for the labors that confront their human family. Inhabitants of the great star nation nurture the minds of their Earth-based counterparts with abundant Love and rich, fruitful hope. We encourage steadfastness in spiritual studies and spiritual activities, for difficult times are yet to be endured before history's final chapter is concluded.

Awakening starseeds are remembering the magnificent worlds where once they lived in light-body form. They are starting to recall the ecstatic sensation of individual consciousnesses coupled in perpetual harmony with One Mind.

As planet Earth moves closer and closer to the lovely interlude of fourth-joining-fifth-octave resonation, beings will begin to experience progressive gradations of bliss. In the early stages, as Earth moves from third-degree into the awakening phases of the astral or fourth-degree octave, their auric fields will begin radiating graceful arcs of expanding light. Those who pledge themselves to personal evolution and the establishment of a new dawn society upon a transformed Earth eagerly await the promise of life immersed in exquisite light.

The beautiful emerald green–sapphire blue planet that adopted humans as her own has served her rowdy, wayward, two-legged offspring well. Never coddling, Earth Mother can be rough in the extreme when she willingly maims or even destroys the physical bodies of her children. Conversely, she gently bathes them in vistas of glorious magnificence and a profusion of rich treasures.

Now her tender hide has become dangerously pockmarked. She is careworn and suffers from battle fatigue. She greatly desires a rest from centuries of selfish acts her children have inflicted upon her. Certainly, she has earned a time to rejuvenate.

Become jubilant with joy! Earth Mother is in the throes of an unprecedented vibrational shift. As her principal caretakers, you must diligently preserve and protect her as graciously as she has always nourished you—providing food, water, clothing, shelter, and the materials from which to mold technology and a worldwide civilization. With a loving, mature attitude, attend to the specifics of your daily chores. You, the starseeds, are prodigal sons and daughters who—some in rebellious ignorance—strayed far from your home stars to seek illusive fortune. Now that you are beginning to remember your way home, gather yourselves before the warm hearth of Earth Mother's voluptuous, protective bosom. Exuberantly sing accolades to your aging adoptive parent who, with great dignity, is about to evolve the harmonics of her planetary hum.

Seeded upon her, you became Earth's children. Now hark unto Tashaba's ancient voice and follow her rich, purring tones as they cascade around you. Scoop up the elements and textures that make up her song, and feast generously upon the luscious texture of its fruity phrases.

Sorrow spent, your day will come. As you wait, hold respect, trust, and faith that the planet's natural vibrancy is evolving its rhythms. Luxuriant nature is Earth's magnificent gown, the coverlet that protects her delicate skin. Humans are the principal handmaidens to this regal queen. As such, cloak her in stately elegance. Soon this jeweled empress will be invited to attend an elaborate ball, a gala celestial event where she is slated to be the honored guest. In preparation, begin to redress her tattered mountains and jungles, her tired seas and worn plains. Transform her so that she sparkles and shines from head to toe when she is called upon to lead the promenade of planets.

Like all great cats, I crouch close to Earth so that I can listen to the deep resonations of her being and clearly discern her heart's melodious hum. For your enjoyment, I have endeavored to illustrate the tonal essence of her powerful song.

Endangered Species

Zoo ship hallways overflow with Earth's flora and fauna, and the crystalline gene pool cubicles are full with DNA imprints of her endangered and extinct animals and plants. Appearing to sleep, they are held in suspended animation awaiting rejuvenation upon a purified, peaceful, light-bodied Earth. However, many species will choose not to return and will opt for revitalization upon planets outside this solar system.

Humans are virtually incapable of comprehending the complex karmic ramifications associated with species extinction. Nevertheless, it will become clear when the evolving segment of the population achieves spiritual maturity. We urge you to review your attitudes and levels of participation in issues associated with debasement of the planet's vitality.

Caretaking duties long performed by mammals who inhabit Earth's majestic oceans escalate, and it is not unusual to find carcasses of whales and dolphins decaying upon beaches. Departing life, they sacrifice themselves for the greater good, dragging their dying bodies onto sandy shores to instill awareness into stubbornly resistant, cosmically blocked humans. Joyfully, we transport their light-bodies home to their native star systems, the peaceful watery worlds of Sirius and the Pleiades.

Succor not the clowns who negatively act out the final scenes of human tragedy, for individuals who focus upon the energy of fear diminish nature's vibrancy. You whose hearts bleed for the return of a pristine, innocent Earth maintain a clearer perspective. You know that plants' and animals' physical bodies are under celestial guidance during life and following death, as are humans'.

Though this essay may be short, do not dismiss it as being unworthy of careful consideration.

Part III: Escalating Songs

Arcturians and Multidimensions

The Arcturians

Arcturians from the Blue Crystal Planet are beings of light. Exactly that. There is no hidden or esoteric meaning in this phrase. We dwell in bliss without suffering the pangs of duality that plague humans.

Human perceptual range is limited to only third-dimensional viewing, although your solar system, like Arcturus, has a third-dimensional component, a fourth-dimensional component, a fifth-dimensional component, and so on. Most star systems associated with extra-terrestrial "phenomena" occurring in third-dimensional Earth space-time are made up of harmonic layers spanning first to ninth dimension. Arcturus is actually a thirteen-dimensional system.

The Blue Crystal Planet is a fifth- and sixth-dimensional planet in the Arcturian star system. Its multi-dimensional harmonics make it an ideal gathering place for multistar beings who serve the Christed Energy for the uplifting of universal vibration throughout this sector of the galactic core. We who communicate with Patricia are situated in fifth- and sixth-harmonic phases. We are preparing for our ascension into seventh and eighth phases in conjunction with Earth's inhabitants rising to fourth and fifth.

Earth's fourth-dimensional spiritual levels are located in the vastness of the multilevel astral planes. All astral travel, out-of-body, dreamtime, and near-death experiences; between-life situations; and spirit guides who resemble humans who have "passed over" (Native American spirits, for example) are Earth space-time fourth-dimensional phenomena. The levels of this plane occupy much universal space. The lower regions are often described as hell or the demonic regions. Its higher levels comprise regions of heavenly bliss and tranquility, the point where harmonic splendor opens upon the raptures of the fifth universal harmonic.

In times of extreme stress, such as a natural disaster, we often manifest as third- or fourth-dimensional energy forms and are often mistaken for angels. Beings of light do resemble angels, but unlike angels, who have never incarnated in physical form, we are like humans in that we, too, must work our way through dimensions.

As Earth's vibratory status refines, paranormal phenomena will appear to be more common, because the energy veil long separating Earth's physical domains from her spiritual domains is dissipating. This delights those of you who dwell in Love. It terrorizes those who dwell in fear.

All planetary systems residing above the higher levels of the fourth dimension dwell in divine bliss, peace, and joy. Think of the lion lying with the lamb. (Lion e lamb is a unique and unholy thought used as an excu third- and lower-fourth-level Dark Lords in some dimensional teaching planets. Their interest is focused upon maintaining Earth's population in a state of terror.)

Communication for beings who dwell at refined vibratory levels is best termed Language of the Sun solar-powered energy. Our bodies comprise shafts of sunlight gathered into form. It is our ecstatic delight to "tune in to" one another through frequencies established through the solar winds and the stellar grids. Traveling along highways of cosmic information, we share as One with that which is not ourselves while remaining ourselves.

Information received by most "civilized" humans in streams of verbal-thought language is due to a deeper respect for brain-mind (mental) intelligence than for heart-mind (intuitive) intelligence. Heart-mind expresses itself through emotional contact with spiritual experiences. Unlike religious training that emphasizes worship of personalities and mental images, deeply meaningful spiritual experiences intuitively connect heart to Soul.

Why is Soul eliminated from your educational systems? For the simple reason that Spirit- or Soul-based systems would strip those who deem themselves "in charge" with no thing to "charge." Spiritual charge is energy or light, fibers of Soul energy that bind all beings in Oneness with Universal Mind, Cosmic Intelligence. Unconditional Love is integrated Cosmic Intelligence manifested as vibrations of sound and light.

Language as symbols is our primary means of active communication with you. True communication is a blending of thought, light, color, sound, and aroma: harmonics of vibration, the music of the stars. That is why you connect to music with such emotional intensity. Verbal and written language opens your brain-minds; music, poetry, and visual art open your heart-minds. Thus, we use human communication to honor your growth and your skill in dynamic persuasion. In so doing, our purpose is to unlock the dormant areas of your Souls, that aspect that remembers why you are on Earth. You have forgotten for a very long time. Now the awakening is upon you. As you awaken, you will remember that you are one of us and have always been so. To illustrate: Palpae and Patricia are droplets in diversity within the waters of the great cosmic ocean. That which is Palpae is a component of Patricia's higher Self. We are multifaceted, multilayered Soul. In a very real sense, Patricia-Palpae is a same-self being. That which is *you* is the same as that which is *us*.

The movie *Cocoon* will aid in your understanding. You are that which we laid down as starseeds. We are those who are reenergizing your light-bodies so you may return fully recovered to your galactic Home. The "old folks" are ancient in Soul-Self. That which is fear is exactly that: one who takes energy that is the rightful will (property) of another.

All things are self-aware. Awareness is not predicated on the level of dimensional achievement. The extent of Soul awareness, however, is predicated on the level of dimensional achievement. For instance, Earth's human population, although extremely self-aware in terms of ego-identification, is virtually comatose in respect to Soul-awareness.

Consciousness of Self is not something that is lost through the act of transposing a physical body into a spirit body. However, consciousness of Soul does not awaken until Soul body fully integrates with spirit body, a feat only the most proficient earthbound spiritual masters have accomplished. Beings who finely resonate as light-entities do not struggle and so remain fully Soul-conscious.

Perhaps a simplification of these issues would be helpful: Energy vibrates at varying rates of speed. Dimensional planes or levels are varying degrees of energy in motion. The primary difference between physical bodies and beings of light is that physical mass vibrates slower than light mass.

Are we energy-conscious of ourselves? Indeed! Are you not also energy-conscious of yourselves? The only difference between us is the level of vibratory perception.

Arcturians could rightly be categorized as spatial philosophers. We serve upon the Regency star council as advisors and manipulators of light within systems like Earth, where darkness threatens the integrity of the planetary body and where Soul species are held captive by beings who prefer darkness to light.

All higher beings are in service. That is a given; that is our purpose. Your purpose also is to serve. In a free-will universe, those who choose light serve Light. Those who choose darkness serve Darkness. To serve is not self-serving, yet it is Self-serving. Service is the only possible way of being.

Service is a given; commitment is not. The degree of commitment establishes the degree of service. Thus, free will is predicated upon level of commitment, not upon service.

Arcturians do not reach back from the future or reach forward from the past. Past, present, and future are illusion. We are in holy Now at all times. That which we are, you are also. That which you are has always been us. The perpetration of the time illusion upon Earth is the chain that must be broken by that which is *you.* Time contains elements of karma. Time contains elements of density (gravity) that hold you captive—even at the spirit level—upon Earth and within the ethereal winds that ply the planet where your Spirit resides between physical lives. Break the illusion of time and you will ascend into the realms of light. In truth, there is no difference or separation of that which is we-you.

Hold tight the essences of time and multiplicity, and you will create karma, which creates density, which creates gravity, which is what captures you and holds you in bondage upon Earth. Simply stated, this is what has occurred upon Earth.

On Oneness

The Arcturians

As you proceed in your investigation of cosmic issues, remain clearly focused. The answer to all questions is *One*. One *is* Divine Principle manifested. We cannot overemphasize that your only real problem is denying your true relationship with God, with That Which Is One. Your greatest challenge, individually and collectively, is to break the captive chains of your negative-based extraterrestrial oppressors.

The Arcturians are in universal service. All beings of higher-octave orders are in service to Universal Harmonic Oneness, and many systems interact with Earth.

Earth is a teaching planet. Arcturians are cosmic teachers and governors of harmonic tranquility. We, among other members of the Regency star council, were instrumental in setting upon Earth ways (as orchestrated by Universal Spiritual Resonance) to establish the permanence of light in human colonies. That which the Arcturians set in place is the imprint of the Oneness of Being. Oneness of Being is a spiritual teaching described in all human religious texts.

Oneness is very difficult for humans to understand. You are adepts at compartmentalization. "This is this" and "that is that" keeps you at arm's length, lest your worship of complexity dare merge into simplicity. You are so enmeshed in the illusionary teachings of third-dimensional reality that you become terrorized at the thought of identity loss. Fear of wholeness (Oneness) is so deeply embedded in your psyches that you prefer to dwell in despair, sorrow, and war-ravaged turmoil rather than to embrace yourselves as diverse drops of cosmic energy bonded in magnificent perpetuity with Omnipresent Mind.

Humans believe there must be a flip side to all things—black-white, dark-light, sad-happy. Our primary goal is to set a grid of Oneness so firmly upon Earth that humans no longer believe energy is something that must be consumed or that the illusion of third-dimensional duality must be maintained.

We are manifestations of Divine Light held in harmonic cadence by the hums of the many planets. That which are inhabitants of the Arcturian star system are billions of light hums resounding as One. We are all One. We do not consider ourselves otherwise. The same with you are we One. The same with Pleiadians and Antarians and Sirians are we One, and so forth and so forth without end. They-we-you are all manifestations of identical Divine Energy. Universal Intelligence—God—is not a substance that is divisible.

When you stop counting in multiples, you will find peace of mind. Numbers are simply fields of energy that ebb and flow. Time is simply fields of energy that ebb and flow. What is confusing to the human mind is that Oneness is capable of diversity of being—many as One.

The Star Councils

Palpae for the Arcturians

Allow your mind to clearly sparkle, Manitu, for I have eagerly awaited our connection. At present, I am "stationed" aboard the intergalactic mother starship, *Marigold–City of Lights*, biblically referred to as New Jerusalem. As a light-bodied resident of the Blue Crystal Planet of Arcturus, I have prepared my I Am-ness to assume Soul-service functions in Earth's solar quadrant. Here the critically grave situation is due to the impact of harmful beings who prey upon the inhabitants of your sun's planet family.

Because of its centralized location upon the star grids, the exquisite Crystalline City of the Blue Crystal Planet is a principal gathering site for representatives of the great star nation to hold star council meetings. However, when council meetings pertain to the delicate situation within Sol's network of planets, beads of grid-patterned lights that link Arcturus to Sol facilitate instantaneous transport of many Arcturian starships to Sol's region. Then the meetings are held on Saturn at the Intergalactic Brotherhood's local starbase and are officiated by the supreme leader of Sol's Spiritual Hierarchy, the Christ Essence, Sananda.

The Law of Free Endeavor is a substrate of Universal Law. All fifth- and sixth-dimensional beings in service to Earth abide by the law's substrates as applicable to each being's will. As such, there is never forced conscription into the Intergalactic Brotherhood. Now that Earth preliminary maneuvering procedures are drawing to a close, all Sol-based Intergalactic Brotherhood members are re-reviewing their Soul energies and willingness for continued participation. (Incidentally, the Intergalactic Brotherhood's length of service to Earth would, most assuredly, astound you.)

To elaborate further upon the vast telepathic communications network that links the minds of light-resonating entities in Oneness with Divine Mind: The star councils serve as a universal governing body. Inhabitants of all sun systems that function under the precepts of intergalactic philosophy and the principles of Divine Law have representatives upon the councils.

Cosmically awakening humans, those who are developing a focused, heart-centered awareness that acknowledges they are coparticipants in wondrous events associated with self and planetary evolution, have begun to sweetly and harmoniously vibrate. Their passionate desire to attain light-body ascension sends beams of light soaring through their crown chakras that transmit a telepathic summons drawing us to them. As they awaken, the star councils will invite them to take their places within the expanding ranks of humans who serve as ground troops for mission Earth evolution: sky warriors, eagles of a new dawn.

Eventually, an evolved Earth population, one that is committed to upholding Divine Omniscient Law, will become fully cognizant of its right to sit upon the councils. The day draws near when a vibrationally refined humanity will send its coordinators to the councils where they will be welcomed as young, energetic beings who vibrate in graceful symmetry with the hum of their parent sun and parent planet.

Elder spiritual masters who have achieved ascension, as well as those still living in physical bodies, have long served Earth as prominent members of the star councils, although you do not generally recognize them. Wise, learned, spiritual people have long understood their roles within the greater cosmos. Spiritual, empowered masters are often unobtrusive teachers whose devoted students greatly honor them for their wisdom and integrity. Unhampered by restrictive, material-world thinking, those who master the spiritual arts evolve a clarity of mind that grants them access to the humming star cords. Like angels they gracefully move through the illusionary webs of temporal time that hold less alert humans captive.

Star council representatives of the Spiritual Hierarchy who direct and coordinate all galactic activities within this universal sector include His Grace, the Christ Essence, Sananda; the archangels and the angelic realm; various light brotherhood orders of ascended and embodied masters; and fifth- and sixth-dimensional light-bodied extraterrestrial beings who make up the Intergalactic Brotherhood of Light. The Arcturians are a subdivision of the Intergalactic Brotherhood of Light.

The star councils maintain a retinue of thousands of starships at all times in and around your solar system. When transmissions are beamed to Patricia through the Arcturian group mind, fifth- and sixth-dimensional vibrational energy is transmitted into the third dimension as a single resonating, synchronized impulse.

Delegates to the star councils represent the energies of the united beings of all galactic sectors within the universe as a whole. Beings who serve Universal Intelligence—God—upon the star councils do so from a place of unconstrained will.

We who represent the collective mind of the star councils suggest you contemplate upon the highest interests of your personal good. As you do so, you may discover a desire to thoroughly peruse the teachings set forth in this manuscript.

Intergalactic entities have established their principal starship maneuver base within your sun system on Saturn. Glorious Saturn moves along her spatial course encapsulated in a brilliant hue of crystalline rings. The vibrational harmonics emitted by Saturn's singing tones are most pleasing to us. When contemplating the delicacy of her magnificent rings, we do not observe hunks of floating rocks or frozen water or gaseous fragments. No indeed! Our exquisitely developed senses tune to the gentle humming florals of her magnificent song.

As we hush the energies of this transmission, we wish to remind you of our esteemed honor and commitment to serve the needs of humans who aspire to spiritual ascension in this lifetime.

As Humans Demolish Earth

Palpae

History has woven a tangled web of negativity about Earth's superb body. Why do humans, whose hearts are so warm and tender, subject themselves to the worship of conclusions based on unyielding logic? Justifying their behavior upon callous, meticulous calculations, your leaders are close to accomplishing an act of suicidal insanity, a demolishing of the vital forces that sustain the health of beautiful Earth.

Surely it is an anomaly that with the diversity of spiritual resources available, humans seem to favor any opportunity to worship the negative impulses of fear rather than their heart-minds' emotional pleas to create a world built on love, harmony, and peace. The sensitive carry an increasing burden of sorrow and despair while the courageous continue to nurture trust and hope that the plants and animals they so dearly love will not slip over the brink to extinction.

Judge, you physicians, the schizophrenia of the people, the splitting of the psyche, the schizoid madness that propels them along their perverse course. The devastating energies of fear permeate their lives. Truly, it is an insane act to consciously choose the evil influence of Dark Lords.

Even our patience wearies at times as we observe the depth of hopelessness that overwhelms those who live their lives vainly searching for Love's sweet promise. Few choose to direct their attention elsewhere. Humans greedy for power and material gain tightly clasp the bridle of Earth chariot in a last, futile attempt to subjugate the people. We strongly warn those of you who persist in playing fear's soon-to-be-outmoded game: The cart your shortsighted, headstrong attitudes drive is headed toward the rim of a dark pit. The light-seeking beings you leave in your wake will be picked up as if on the wings of eagles and flown to the stars.

As always, the media are replete with atrocities that humans unceasingly perpetrate upon one another. There is no justification for treacherous behavior, and the Spiritual Hierarchy will not be satisfied with lame, childish excuses.

We have come to Earth to harvest our crops—the precious starseeds. The day nears for us to bundle them up and transport them Home. However, understand that any being who wishes to remain spirit-connected to Earth's delightful energies will, one fine day, observe Sol shining upon a rosy-hued world, an Earth at peace, an Earth free from disease and war.

Awakening humans resemble pearls. Their gem-quality auras exude radiant showers of effervescent light beside the whines of the disillusioned and downtrodden. Nevertheless, Earth glows with joyous energies that light-seeking humans emit. Truly, the awakening are among the bravest of the brave. The spiritually courageous have not lost hope and faith that all will soon be well, though their hearts are often ravished with grief. The light that pours from these wondrous beings is wattage power.

We come close to Earth riding upon our mother ship, magnificent *Marigold–City of Lights*. *Marigold*'s mighty girth hovers unseen above you. Were we to unveil her bulk, you would be unable to view the sun over much of the North American continent. Vast! Vast indeed is exquisite *Marigold*.

Palpae transmits at the request of the Arcturian star council. Arcturians in residence Earth sector appreciate the opportunity to serve under the auspices of the Christ Essence, Sananda. His Essence directs all intergalactic gatherings held upon *Marigold–City of Lights*, doubt this not!

Holocausts and the Law of Free Endeavor

PALPAE

This narrative will cover barely understood parameters that have determined Earth's vibrational placement within the cosmos. Though Earth primarily functions at third-dimensional resonation, she retains some second-dimensional undertones and also incorporates some refined, fourth-dimensional overtones. For example, second-dimensional undertones includes flat tones of black and white; depth of color and shape occur in the third-dimensional planes. When humans travel out of body in the fourth dimension, form takes on dreamlike qualities.

Prior to the advent of humanlike creatures upon Earth, the Regency star council defined a physical environment where certain "unruly" elements from several star systems could be placed for careful monitoring. Thus, Earth (as well as other places) was set aside as a local quarantine district where entities wishing to indulge themselves in solar war games could play at will without damaging the galaxy's more peaceful inhabitants. Many God-forsaking beings are still encamped there on a semipermanent basis, that is, until they will themselves to radiate light.

In addition, Earth serves as a teaching planet for newly birthed Souls, as a recharge center for old Souls, and as a fertile training ground for Souls desiring to evolve from a "me only" attitude, which originally brought many of them there. And to assist in Earth's evolution, spiritual warriors from many star systems volunteered to descend into physical matter to maintain and protect planetary equilibrium.

Long before the rise of human civilization—and there have been other civilizations before this one—an invasion of extraterrestrials came to Earth to carve out a slave empire they proposed to rule without interference from the star councils. They set out to capture the budding human species in a web of suspicion and intrigue. Ill-gotten technology enabled them to set up and maintain a force field of negative magnetic attraction around the planet that stopped Earth's positive-oriented beings from experiencing spiritual growth. They used a chemical agent best described as cosmic swamp gas to overcome unwary Souls and place them in a subordinate, slumberlike state.

Shortly after their arrival, the invaders began squabbling among themselves while attempting to secure the coveted position of Dark Lords' dictator. Mimicking their behavior, humans became caught up in a succession of intertribal conflicts, culminating, in current times, in a plague of world wars and nationalistic states. Science fiction views extraterrestrial invasion as a distinct probability.

In reality it is a fait accompli, for Earth's citizens long since chained themselves to the rule of Dark Lords.

Dark Lords maintain themselves through a system of rules based upon the premise that I and we must enslave you and them. The beginning of their horrific reign resulted in the advent of dinosaurs and other life forms that began a feeding frenzy which continues unabated to this day.

To clarify the term *feeding frenzy*, understand that all life has the ability to absorb energy for sustenance from the cosmic air. However, because of the invaders' manipulations, all Earth creatures (animals in particular, though plant forms were involved as well) found it necessary to constantly protect their preestablished hunting and feeding grounds.

Now we come to the question of why history is replete with mass murders known as holocausts. In a free-will universe, the Law of Free Endeavor allows negativity, but it is kept closely confined by the Spiritual Hierarchy. Because of this law, we are not permitted to interfere in human affairs unless our assistance is specifically requested through the transmissions of your thoughts.

The Law of Free Endeavor also allows all planetary systems to establish themselves as they will, subject to the karmic Law of Cause and Effect. However, beings living upon light-refined worlds have overcome the necessity for cosmic intervention in a similar way university graduates have moved beyond the regulatory encumbrances that, by necessity, must bind the choices of school-age children.

Hitler's slaughter was a direct result of an accumulation of murderous energies arising from holocausts occurring throughout human development. Although holocausts are truly terrible—the worst form of evil—advancing Souls are able to take advantage of heightened energies associated with group death by using them to secure their Souls' permanent release from karmic Earth bondage.

To heal holocaust atrocities at your emotional, heart level, you must understand that in reality all humans are components of Soul energy. Each of you is an eternal being temporarily housed in a physical body. However, many Souls are less evolved than others. For this reason the Spiritual Hierarchy confines many Souls to Earth to ensure peaceful harmonics within the light-vibrating realms. A great many advanced Souls are there as well, having volunteered to descend into matter to establish and serve Divine Will upon Earth.

We reiterate that you are living in an accelerated, transitional era. Much jockeying for galactic position is occurring, for Dark Lords remain entranced with the trappings of pseudopower and intend to continue enslaving unaware Soul energies. Throughout the twentieth century they have focused their efforts to ensnare as much lower-state Soul energy as possible, for they intend to continue status quo after they are removed to a lower-vibrational universe.

It is imperative for your well-being to understand that although some group deaths are the result of evil practices, many incidents of multiple death, such as those resulting from "accidents" and acts of nature, are used by the Spiritual Hierarchy to release many Souls simultaneously, as permitted within their prelife contracts. We do not mean to imply that things which appear evil are not evil. Those who awaken to higher cosmic reality already comprehend that death is an illusion, but the majority continue to struggle at the gut level in an attempt to differentiate good intention from evil intention. The ability to discern all things as Soul in progress is a vital step in your long road to galactic maturation.

The Mysteries

Palpae

It is common for humans to become bewildered when confronted with the presence of anything they cannot logically explain. But few escape the proddings of their naturally inquisitive minds. Though inexplicable happenings are seldom a topic of discussion in polite society, humans are curious and fascinated with the unknown.

Teaching devices used by fifth- and sixth-dimensional beings to awaken you to a greater view of reality may be tucked into whatever narrow pigeonholes you choose. Certainly, we are aware that most consider the possibility of extraterrestrial life extremely suspect, let alone that such oddities may be intelligent, spiritual, and peaceful.

Beings who serve the Intergalactic Brotherhood of Light are stationed in Earth's spatial regions for explicit purposes. It is not an aspect of our natures to be secretive, and our motivations and methods are well outlined in many "channeled" materials rapidly becoming available throughout much of human society.

For a moment, set aside the notion that UFOs containing buggy-eyed slimy-green monsters may be hovering above you, for the authenticity of extraterrestrials is not the primary theme of this essay. Our point is that due to Earth's refining energies it is urgently necessary for you to vastly widen your perceptions of reality. We challenge you to evolve your traditional third-dimensional viewpoints to embrace a much broader universal cosmology.

The seas and skies are rich with flavors and scents of wondrous things full of life's abundance, though you are limited in your ability to directly partake of all their rich ingredients. Securely captured by the chains of duality, your experience for the most part has comprised long periods of spiritual, emotional, physical, and even mental isolation. Most take little time in the busy-ness of their days to explore their internal natures, and they maintain only a perfunctory knowledge of their true Selves and those of their families and friends. As a whole, humans have never experienced the perfection, the exquisite joy that is the expression of peaceful, spiritually uplifted, harmoniously unified people. Compassionate beings who reside outside your star system view the human drama as unnecessarily tragic.

Recent breakthroughs in technology, particularly in network communications, have shrunk your once-private-self world. Few places remain where your neighbors' business cannot be comfortably observed from your television and computer screens. Therefore, whenever you become overwhelmed with anxiety and are confronted with the uncomfortable prospects of a mysterious future, we urge you to move beyond mindless forms of entertainment you are prone to use for escape. We submit it would better serve you to investigate the deeper truths behind the events that dominate the evening news. Rise to a higher viewpoint and obtain a clearer insight into the alarming circumstances that threaten the natural environment and human society with catastrophe. Although it remains true you cannot ignore the fact that the natural vitality of Earth's flora, fauna, water, land, and air hover on the edge of bankruptcy—and we continue to encourage you to take immediate action to remedy this perilous situation—we also urge you to understand that there are highly spiritual reasons for the escalation of the troublesome energies that plague you.

To facilitate your growth beyond the narrow margins of third-dimensional physical reality, we ask that all diligent, multidimensional telepaths record the evolutionary situation as simply and as persuasively as possible. As you find spiritually inspired writings being released from higher-resonating worlds, you will discover our remarks in many places.

Amass all the splendid writings the multidimensional telepaths are gathering. May the format of these constantly evolving publications comfortably introduce you to your family from the stars. Treasure all your "channeled" books, for galactially inspired writings are as precious as the oats, wheat, and barley representative of Earth Mother's abundance. Joyously read the pages until you clearly understand every nuance of every sentence. Note that the contents of all fifth-, sixth-, and higher-dimensional "channeled" books approach you with gentle Love. Bruise not their beautiful contours with elements of distrust and scorn. Protect and cherish each transmission that comes your way. Information telepathically plucked from the subtle octaves represents another human's commitment to universal cause and to be of service to the human family.

We do not expend our energy to captivate professors of philosophy, captains of industry, leaders of nations, or the economically privileged. From stars to Earth, we reach down to lovingly embrace those who are the foundation of human society. Take time to seek us out. Persistently question all proficient telepaths who come your way. As you do so, you will notice an underlying message: Starship residents have issued an invitation to the people of Earth to become One with the greater galactic community. Additionally, as you broaden the scope of your spiritual work, your psychic aptitudes will begin to bubble to the surface. Move steadily and persistently along your path, and never despair or indulge yourself in comparing your abilities with those of another.

Like Patricia, if you are among those challenged to telepathically record and distribute multidimensional information on a broad scale, you, too, will be similarly requested to share the gifts you have received. As you do so, emulate her efforts to freely divulge the wondrous things she has learned with all who approach her sincerely. All who feel compelled from the depths of their heart-minds' understanding are among those summoned to perform their Souls' greatest works.

Tools of Our Trade

Palpae

Behold the nature of light that is ours to command: the tools of our trade, the rainbow-hued optical wonders of purples, blues, oranges, yellows, pinks, violets, greens, and reds. As we urge Earth's vibrations to a higher resonating frequency, crystalline starship "lasers" regularly crisscross and caress her body with sweetly scented, subtly hued, humming ethereal light.

Vortices are regions of whirling energy (light) where grid points converge. Powerfully charged vortices are strategically positioned along the rims of the continents' tectonic plates. These vortices are principal focal points for gathering and harmonizing currents that threaten the stability of the planetary grids. However, because it is limited to third-dimensional observation, human science is at a loss to explain the periodic disappearances that plague geographic areas where these vortices are located. From our point of view, it would appear reasonable, even logical (to use your favorite term), to attribute much of these phenomena to extraterrestrial activity.

For example, many are familiar with the strange incidents associated with the Bermuda Triangle. The triangle is a massive, powerful vortex situated upon the focal point of the greater Atlantic grid. Because it is the nature of energy to expand and contract, from time to time the triangle widens to such an extent that it creates an exceptionally large space-time portal. When this occurs, ships and planes are drawn through the portal and their occupants find themselves face-to-face with inhabitants of fifth- and sixth-dimensional starships.

As Earth moves into the window when her body undergoes transdimensional exchange, the Bermuda Triangle vortex will increase until it touches the widening Lemurian vortex (located atop the greater Pacific grid). Points where the two vortices touch will exude brilliant, ultraradiant light. As they conjoin in mutual harmonic agreement, Earth will peacefully slide into her birth canal and be delivered into the refined realms of light-bodied planets.

Highly charged vortices occasionally open interdimensional doorways that provide starships with third-dimensional access. When we move through these doorways, we lower our ships' vibrations until they assume physical (third-dimensional) appearance. These visitations account for some, but certainly not all, UFO reports in which our ships appear to humans as metal craft. However, fifth- and sixth-dimensional starships are not manufactured from metals but are created from by-products of thought merged with the clicking hum of crystals.

One of our major endeavors as planet healers is to maintain ocean energy portals and vortices in perpetual, peaceful bliss. To perform this critically important task, banks of crystalline "lasers" on starships send streams of multicolored light Earthward, where they are absorbed by gigantic, light-emitting crystalline pyramids located deep in the oceans. Though ethereal, ocean-based pyramids are not visible to humans, they are maintained in peak hum capacity by specially trained dolphins and whales. Whale minds are particularly adept at this function; these magnificent cetaceans serve as pyramid information coordinators.

These brief sentences were designed to clarify at least one enigma that has long perplexed curious humans. It is our purpose to help you understand that mysterious disappearances ascribed to the Bermuda Triangle are, in reality, nothing more frightening than a magnificent doorway into the beauteous Plains of Perpetual Resonation. Portals to Peace would be an excellent analogy. So I say and quite sincerely do I mean.

Space Travel and Galactic Contracts

Palpae

Impulsively driven to explore Earth's uncharted regions, you incessantly prowl around your planet like panthers on a hunt. Persistently challenged by the great unknown, pulled by your minds' unlimited capacity to imagine, your free-ranging thoughts touch down onto worlds of alternative realities. Elusive, shimmering cities sparkling with jewels and tapestries tantalize your visionary eyes with sights your physical eyes have never seen. The creative centers of your productive, dreaming minds are replete with wondrous creatures and colorful reflections your Soul brings forth from its collection of timeless Memories. Deep within you are hungry to escape the horizons of your limited senses.

You are now becoming aware that the stars are summoning you, and their tantalizing songs tug at you. You know you have begun a process of personal evolution that will culminate in your being welcomed aboard the starships by members of your light-family.

In preparation for unencumbered travel in the higher realms, you must first learn to recognize the subtle nuances of your inner voices and acknowledge the luminescent visions that spark your heart-minds' desires. You must carefully cultivate an overwhelming urge to live a holy, saintly life. Before you are allowed access onto the interstellar pathways, you must make the long, often difficult journey that leads to ultimate self-mastery.

Until humans learn to discern the landscapes of the inner worlds, they will be limited to traveling through space in cumbersome metallic cans. They will be reduced to laboring on the surfaces of planets and moons while encased in plastic and rubber apparel. So trite, so restricting! Freedom is denied only because humans fear the ramifications of responsible cosmic citizenship.

Eventually, our crystalline ships will fly humans who make a choice for light ascension to the stars. Commitment to attain spiritual mastery is a primary focus of the galactic contract, which will bring evolved humans into perpetual Oneness with the multidimensional residents of the great star nation. This contract is binding and its simple tenets are based on universal Love. Seeking humans are already more or less cognizant of the nature of the contract. Certainly, documents generated by the star councils and the Spiritual Hierarchy contain no secrets for the sole benefit of priests, presidents, and kings. The covenant between occupants of the star councils and evolving Earth inhabitants will be agreed upon by individuals, free will intact, prior to their welcome into the greater cosmic community as fully participating citizens.

Multidimensional data are not being telepathed to glorify the egos of a select few. Ability to directly communicate with beings of light is the right, indeed the responsibility, of all cosmically aware beings. We who inhabit the luminescent worlds do not live vicariously. No indeed. The eyes of our Souls are doorways into other universes.

The finely chiseled lines of this essay originate in the Arcturian star fields. Carefully cherish our comforting words, for they outline songs the stars sing and the poetic stanzas of light-humming planets.

On Suns

Quantra

Many humans have the notion that more often than not planetary systems revolve around a single sun. This, however, is a concept that is not entirely based upon fact. For example, the Arcturian star system is home to two major suns. Giant, rosy Arcturus, our predominant sun, can be seen by the naked eye as one of the brightest stars in Earth's night sky. The diminutive Arcturian white sun, although much larger than your Sol, can be seen only by light-dimension beings.

Eventually, Jupiter's nature to become a sun will reveal itself. Although your scientific community has gathered much data that hint of mighty Jupiter's greater purpose, it has not yet discovered that within Jupiter is a restless core of energy that parallels solar density mass.

Here and there in the recordings given to Patricia is information on the esoteric ingredients of sun chemistry.

Throughout these writings we often allude to the spiritual composition of suns. We arranged this material as simply as possible to give you important reference points so you can expand your knowledge of the divine nature of suns and their service to their planetary families.

In one of our initial transmissions to Patricia, Palpae confirmed his origins when he stated, "I speak to you from cloud tunes of the red sun." This was done to trigger into awareness the mechanics of her DNA cell structures that hold her Soul Memories. Like Patricia, many humans devoted to Divine Truth are Soul-connected Arcturian starseeds.

Red, rosy Arcturus is the warmth and glory of the Arcturians' existence. Around her generous solar body, the diminutive, dense white sun rides the cosmic waves as Arcturus's satellite. As best as can be described for human understanding, the white sun functions as a protector or "masculine" solar source for the more "feminine" Arcturian red star and her planetary children.

The humming vibrations sung by the two Arcturian suns balance and harmonize the united Oneness that is representative of the entire Arcturian star system.

Clarifying Comments from Palpae

As a solar scientist, Quantra's abilities are held in high esteem by we who reside upon the Arcturian planets. In accord with his Soul's primary, specialized purpose, Quantra retrieves, distributes, and monitors energies of the solar hum. His immeasurable generosity of spirit has brought him to Earth environs to aid in the enlightenment of dedicated, evolving humans.

Arcturian solar-bank data are always accessible to any Arcturian citizen who seeks them out. However, the tonal resonations of a being of synergized light, such as Quantra, accelerate the absorption of streams of solar energies into silolike crystal generator "think tanks," which serve Arcturians as communication network power centers. Simply put, Quantra's specialized vibrations strum at a pitch that enhances the melodic strands Arcturian suns naturally hum.

Interstellar beings communicate via Language of the Suns, the rhythmic telepathic hums that vocalize the stars. Cosmic telepathy is a process of wrapping one's mind with Omnipotent Intelligence, whose archives are stored in stars. Solar communication grids are useful for contacting awakening beings who are new to the telepathic process. Earth's sun, Sol, is a vast storehouse of divinely inspired knowledge and is a common denominator between humans and the residents of fifth- and sixth-dimensional starships.

Omnipotent Creator's omnipresent wisdom has provided Its children with a vast star-to-star, galaxy-to-galaxy, universe-to-universe communication web. As you learn to connect your thoughts to the sun's grid link to Arcturus, the Pleiades, and beyond, you will find you have achieved instantaneous access to a vast telecommunication network that is hindered neither by space nor by time.

We realize that it may take a great deal of intellectual reshuffling before you are entirely able to grasp the concept that suns are computerlike storehouses of infinite knowledge. Though suns are certainly not gods to be worshiped as such, they are worthy of a mightier respect than technology-loving humans are willing to grant them.

Using light-generating creative visualization, you will soon learn that the sun's powerful, well-stocked library is available to all well-intentioned beings.

The phrases of this essay on suns may ring strangely to your ears. To be told of fantastic, faraway places and incomprehensible beings for which your minds have no points of reference may seem vague and elusive, like childhood dreams. In spite of this, with Patricia's agreeable assistance, we will continue to deposit many wondrous images throughout our writings.

Humanity's Dual Nature

Palpae

Allow your visionary mind to dwell upon our peaceful, loving essences. We are formed of liquid light; we are as delicate as molten gold. Our starships vibrate like tinkling silver bells. Increasingly, you find yourself pulled toward the graceful starships that your growing awareness is drawing down from the stars. You have begun to snuggle into hope's elegant warmth as if nestled in the depths of a cozy blanket while the winds of winter pile snow upon the land.

Many resist the arrival of starships as relentlessly as they attempt to avoid the terrifying prospects of an out-of-control future by cowering before it in fear. We gently remind you: avoidance behavior is not in your best interest. Fear of responsibility, *and all that implies*, in reality is your only enemy.

You who opt for evolutionary at-One-ment and lightbody ascension are advised to accelerate the rate of your inward journeys. Make an earnest effort to rediscover your innocent selves by recalling the glorious days of carefree childhoods. Your childlike qualities hold the key to unlocking the portals of your Souls. Conjure up youthful visions, a time when your thoughts held not a care for world economics, the state of national politics, or wages to be earned. Your child-selves seek out butterflies and moths. Your child-selves yearn for hot summer days and squishing toes in muddy banks and minnow-filled streams.

A balanced life contains a mixture of spring's eternal promise, some blush from summer's flower gardens, a toss or two of autumn's unique spirit, and a dash of winter's cold breath. Your child-selves know that summer's heat and winter's cold are but one and the same, opposite sides of an identical coin. The changing seasons are Earth's way of maintaining a proper balance within her dynamic energies.

In many ways, humanity's unstable temperament mirrors the fluctuating rhythms of its planetary home. One facet of human duality reflects its dark side, the terrifying aspects of shadowy night. The other facet reflects humanity's day side, which embraces qualities of high Love and radiates properties of Divine Light. The constant interplay of evil (negative) energies and good (positive) energies within the individual and collective consciousness creates an ongoing destructive-constructive situation within Earth's sphere of cosmic influence. A primary reason your Soul incarnated upon this yin-yang planet was so it could experience the evolutionary dynamics within the energy polarities of an accelerating-decelerating world.

To master spiritual integrity, sooner or later you must directly confront the lowest and meanest features of your ego's two-sided nature. To challenge the shadowy world of your wounded psyche and bestow compassion's sweet kiss upon it is to give honor to your dark side. An act of compassion for yourself is karmically transformative. As all true healers understand, before they can restore their patients to prime health they must first initiate self-healing treatments. Healers cannot fully appreciate the suffering of others until they acknowledge their own inner torments. To see oneself nakedly is to understand another absolutely.

As lovingly and as gently as possible, we inform you that humans have only two remaining options: they must either self-determine or they will self-destruct. As things stand, a majority are stuck in a state of advanced spiritual decline. Self-imposed spiritual inertia is a serious matter on a Soul level. Those who turn their backs upon the call to acknowledge their divine natures are rapidly accumulating a deleterious amount of karmic debris. On a brighter note, those who are resolutely working to master personal and spiritual integrity have plotted a heady course that will eventually culminate in their ascending to light-body status.

We encourage you to undertake self-transformation. Let go of your periodic fits of dark despair. That which is written is attainable. Although it remains true that a concerted effort at physical, emotional, and mental self-disciple is required for light-body maturation, the energy dynamics of these evolutionary times make it possible for all determined seekers to transcend all dense layerings of karmic residue.

The trails the Spiritual Hierarchy are blazing around the world are neither obscure nor hidden. The path Home is well marked and all may traverse it. As you perform the mundane tasks of your daily lives, you are never alone. Beings of light float within easy reach whenever you request their assistance. Certainly, it is becoming increasingly difficult to ignore what is, quite frankly, exceedingly obvious.

Transmitted via the intelligence of the solar grid, this message stands complete.

Adonai.

Human Defiance, Human Glory

PALPAE

Harmonious living plays few chords in turbulent times. On a cosmic scale, the situation upon Earth has grievous connotations.

Humanity's rebellious defiance of Universal Law is graphically portrayed in its perpetual fascination with the accoutrements of war. The dove of peace seldom, if ever, hovers over the people of your planet. Becoming excited at the prospects of battle and death is truly the mark of a primitive species.

Human leaders wear tarnished crowns when an essentially noble people emit only an occasional gasp of glorious potential. The most powerful rulers of Earth's mightiest nations have either forgotten or are deliberately undermining the original intent of their countries' founders. Fearful of a greater vision, they are driven by shortsighted wealth and power. Greed that benefits only a select few serves to the detriment of the many.

Earth's rugged face is aged and worn. She tires of her human children's immature, frigid quarrels. Few grasp the full impact of ignoring spiritual disciplines. Divine teachings were not set down in ancient times for intellectual discussion by the philosophically astute. The intention of sacred writings is to illustrate the way cosmically mature beings live.

Here and there on Earth are a growing number of "unnoticed" ones. Those silent folk hold humanity's fate in their humble hands. Those whose tongues refuse to spew discontent and anger into the winds, though their hearts are full of sorrow, are destined to transform the world.

The spiritually courageous are moving further and further away from the ill-trod path favored by those who persist in clinging to fear. Layers of thick karmic residue are peeling off the awakenings' spirit-bodies and are dropping by the wayside.

Prophets have alluded to the humans who seek enlightenment during massive Earth changes as rainbow warriors, members of the family of light. We refer to these marvelous beings as wanderers, sky warriors, eagles of the new dawn. Spiritually dedicated humans share a grassroots commonality and will eventually merge in sacred Oneness with the greater galactic community.

In August 1987 a major alteration in Earth's wattage power took place at the time of the Harmonic Convergence. Energies arising from the world peace meditation held in that transformative year were so profound that they precipitated a significant negative-to-positive polarity shift in Earth's physical and etheric body. Since then, people who perceive themselves as being "in charge" of the world's decision-making processes have become more and more confused. Though they cling to teetering positions of vapid authority, Earth's royal scepter has been taken from their generally incompetent hands and has been placed firmly into the hands of those who are humble. As prophesied, the meek are to inherit the Earth. Those who radiate love and light are fast coming into their own. Mark these words: Their intent is to lighten your load with a message of glad tidings, not to cause you to bend further under the leaden effects of buried shame and barely concealed sorrow.

The day will arrive when the many torments that drain your hearts will seem as if they belonged to a forgotten tale from a long-ago time. In the coming millennium, the unhappy memories of a difficult past will no longer disturb you.

The year 1987 was indeed momentous, a year that sparked a new meaning to the phrase "in the Year of Our Lord." Holy of Holies, the Christed One returns! Recognized throughout the great star nation as Sananda, Being of Infinite Grace, He is busy plucking out the thorns that torture your hearts. Gentle as a soft spring day, He caresses you with salves as rich and ripe as summer's sweetest berries. He anoints your sorrows with liquid golden lights as fresh as blooming daffodils.

This transmission is now emptied of all its fine phrases.

Humans and Earth

Palpae

This essay contains simply stated, well-known scientific facts. Though you may prefer to bumble along your way, blind and unwilling to listen to the details of impending ecological disaster, your planet's needs are no longer something you can afford to ignore.

Solutions for transforming the environment to a state of health are predicated upon human intention, motivation, attitude, and activity. Surely you are aware that you are confronted with the imminent danger of environmental collapse. Emergency procedures are urgently required! A halfhearted attempt to prop up the existing norm is most assuredly not in your best interest. We strongly recommend that you adopt a clearer vision and create unique ways to peacefully solve centuries-old problems. Dance no longer the waltz of a bygone era. As you attempt to make do with yesteryear's methods, you only befuddle yourselves and accomplish very little in the way of effective, tangible results. As you study the manuals in this series, you will find many suggestions outlining ways you may accomplish these difficult tasks.

Clever humans, must the devil be on your doorstep before you willingly surrender yourselves to a higher purpose? Are you not aware that there lurks a malignant evil intent on enslaving you? Dark Lords are most effective at focusing your interest toward mass hysteria and spiritual disinterest. The disfigurements they weave are neither more nor less destructive than your reluctance to institute, at the very least, a dynamic trial and error approach to your predicaments. Vigorously reconstruct a society that will reflect Divine Creator's abundant energies. Pull out all stops! Plunge courageously ahead.

You are at a crossroads in evolutionary development. Humans no longer walk the same road down time's long corridor. Obvious signposts that mark the point of divergence escape the notice of those who rush ahead with their spiritual eyes snapped securely shut. The awakening are astute enough to know they have attained at least some degree of comprehension. They are quickly learning to keep a close check on their navigational guides, for they know that the time for definitive action is now.

Instructional materials prepared for you by the Intergalactic Brotherhood originate from Prime Directive as mandated by Earth Operations Supreme Commander, the Christ Essence, Sananda. He Who Covers Earth with Light is known throughout the world by many names, among them Jesus, Buddha, Krishna. Ultimate avatar for this solar sector, He is always present to teach, to comfort, and to meet the needs of all people, in all places, at all times. Many will repudiate this statement with a charge of blasphemy. In so doing, they limit the ability of Omnipotent Source to serve all beings in a manner that is suited to their personal dispositions and spiritual needs, no matter their home star, planet, form, or dominant cultural system.

Your spiritual requirements are as unique as your preferences in mates, food, and homes. But readers who study the sacred writings of all human belief systems soon discover an underlying commonality permeating all teachings. The powerful priesthoods that gained control over the world's religions have superimposed layers of specialized dogma upon religion's common foundational elements. But basic instruction is that Prime Universal Intelligence manifests Prime Love. Unconditional Love is the *only* teaching. Love without qualification. Love without even the slightest whiff of self-other dissonance.

Cosmic instruction manuals currently manifested into physical form throughout the world are, for the most part, fairly easy to comprehend. Yet most of you will continue to ignore whatever causes discomfort and, more's the pity, argue that it is preferable to proceed at status quo speed. The collapse of institution-based society is imminent. A bleak chapter in the pages of your painful history is rapidly drawing to a close; a brilliant new one is about to begin.

The position we take with you is one of complete challenge. Nothing less! As you accept responsibility for sustained harmonious planetary maintenance, a great deal will be gained. The time has come for you to take concerted, accelerated action. An immediate arousal of the sleeping masses would be so powerful that in one second's time Earth Mother's crippled countenance would heal.

Do not suppose you can leave these matters unattended for your children to face. By then it will be far too late. The harvesting of the starseeds will be complete and starships will have come and gone. Those who persist in ignoring the demands that accompany commitment to spiritual growth will find themselves, in the not-too-distant future, rocking in a creaking old chair in a place that startles not this sun's rays.

Being of serious countenance, the energies of this transmission lack poetry in expression. Our words hang loose and heavy. Be that as it may, for as an intergalactic ambassador to Earth it is my responsibility to so inform you.

A View on the "Art" of War

Arcturian Star Council

Against a backdrop of a setting sun, envision a silhouette of millions upon millions of bloody, ghostly men, women, and children—the horrifying reality of the carnage that pervades human history. Humans focus much attention upon the so-called art of war. The underlying premise is that it is both honorable and glorious to sacrifice one's life to benefit one's country. We observe that the majority who face mutilation and death upon the fields of battle are of what you term lower-class status or rank. This should be clearly understood.

When a human spirit is trapped in violent death and finds itself caught in abrupt physical-to-etheric transformation, it is often ill-prepared to traverse the veil between the material and astral worlds. A newly released spirit can either dissipate or absorb an extraordinary amount of energy as it negotiates the critical path into the astral realms. If the spirit departing its physical body is not completely aware of the purpose of its journey, or if it is expressing anger or desperation, spiritual energy available to it at the moment of transition is greatly reduced or even lost.

Every act of aggression, even though your societies condone it in institutional law, lessens the magnitude of light available to a spirit in transition. Although Prime Law grants all third-dimensional beings the right to break their prelife contracts, advancement of their Souls is predicated upon applying principles of unconditional Love. Unconditional Love energy is not something that can be exploited or divided into categories.

Hostile behavior, no matter how aptly humans justify it, plunges both aggressor and victim into a swirling pool of karmic life-death recycling, creating a pattern of cause-and-effect instability. And although it is rare for the "privileged in rank" to hurl a spear or pull a trigger during battle, those who propel their nations into war greatly exceed their soldiers in accumulating karmic imbalance.

The tool that aligns the Soul's imbalance into harmonious agreement is applied Love for self and others. Recycling continues until such time as a being creates a physical life of purposeful application of Universal Law.

You who are seriously interested in achieving light-body ascension in this lifetime are encouraged to be conscientious objectors if you are asked to perform any activity that is potentially harmful to another being. Therefore, take a courageous stand and do not allow yourselves to be overcome by those who would force you into any form of violent confrontation. Steer clear of involving yourselves in any situation that would damage your Souls, even to the drastic point of giving up your physical body for the integrity of your Soul bodies. Remember, your physical bodies are transitory, but your Souls are eternal.

Earth is unique in its warlike activities. From biblical times to the advent of the nuclear age there is little (if any) observable alteration in humanity's proclivity for establishing military societies. Your preference for aggressive behavior generates repetitive cause-and-effect energies upon all Earth's population. Generation after generation has deviated little from this pattern of reincarnating. From our point of view, it appears pointless that you remain adamant against creating simple solutions that would establish lasting world peace. Meanwhile, your heinous weapons grow exceedingly monstrous.

Human leaders, if you wish to have starships suddenly materialize over your cities, push the buttons that will unleash nuclear holocaust upon your people. If you unleash your grim weapons, on that day the Intergalactic Brotherhood's policy of nonintervention will become null and void, and our starship fleet will salute you in a manner most are psychologically unprepared to face.

Arcturian representatives of the Intergalactic Brotherhood's Earth harmonic restoration team are familiar with life-to-life recycling. Arcturians in service to humans as guides completely understand your struggles. Before achieving light-body status, we, too (some quite recently), had to conquer the vibrational pull of heavier dimensions.

Eventually, we began to perpetually manifest high Love energy and assume robes of finely spun, radiant light.

Our words are gruffly spoken in order to urgently nudge you into a higher state of cosmic knowledge. We are filled with a deeper love for you than you can imagine. We gaze sadly from our hovering sky seats, for you are our family, you are sleeping citizens of the great star nation. It is most difficult to chastise you, for it is not our wish to deal with our beloved human family in a harsh or unkind manner. Nevertheless, if it appears that our words are devoid of Love-Light expression and infringe upon your right to free will, be that as it may.

We extend compassionate Love's energies to you. It is not pleasurable to our Onenesses to observe you tossing sorrowfully from life to life.

Squander Not the Earth

Palpae

The wise know that the effort put into the pleasant task of nurturing and comforting others is equal to what is received in return. But if you systematically squander the patience and good will of your precious friends and relations, you will soon be alone.

Your selfish, inconsiderate displays toward others mirror the squandering of Earth's precious resources. Humans exhibit an inordinate propensity to abuse Earth Mother. They explode bombs upon her tender skin, they spray her with pesticides, they mold her gracious lines into awkward contours, they stab and poke at her with picks and drills, they cut great swaths through her forests, they commit mayhem upon her creatures, and they lace her delicate hide with the noxious residue of their industrial pollutants. You must ask yourselves if a truly intelligent species would arrogantly destroy the health and well-being of their planet home in such a manner.

Earth's vibrant nature has become caught in the grip of insatiable human greed. As if a serious memory lapse was taking place in their thinking compartments, the majority of humans seldom take time to ponder upon such a worrisome thing as impending worldwide environmental collapse. Westernized humans are particularly entranced with providing themselves with a luxuriant lifestyle and are almost completely absorbed in this pleasant endeavor.

Nevertheless, we persevere in issuing our challenge to you: Become acutely aware whenever you step upon the forest's delicious greenery and the delicate ferns that reside therein. Tenderly and lovingly caress the surface of the oceans so that you do not bruise the sweet bodies of your marvelous cousins who inhabit the seas.

It may not have escaped your notice that these essays appear to be repetitive. This is done in a manner that resembles, but does not entirely replicate, repeating melodies. We find you to be particularly resistant creatures. Our attempts to encourage you to undertake a project as radical as a complete world overhaul requires considerable effort. We assure you that in spite of your hesitancy to play an active role in helping the Spiritual Hierarchy restructure Earth to a lighter vibration, you will, nevertheless, soon observe that what you view as solid reality has become as illusive as floating dust.

Your skyscrapers sustain themselves by reaping a heavy toll upon Earth's rapidly dwindling resources. But by using tools and materials that require only the sublimest energy, you can begin to change your architecture and retool your transportation devices. As you evolve, you will find it neither pleasing nor attractive to live and work in dismal, rigidly shaped buildings. Though you may try to fool yourselves into thinking you are perfectly content residing in a polluted world, your higher Selves do not rest easy when you sustain your lives by debasing Earth's comfort and health. Like a mother's rich, flowing abundance to her babe, a hospitable Mother Earth will provide for her beloved offspring.

Quantum leaps are required and you are rapidly running out of time. Hesitate no longer! In the future you will shake your heads at your reluctance to leave so many displeasing things behind. A chuckle or two will rise as you recall your stubbornness in letting them go.

Prepare space within your homes to gather writings, books, music, videos, and other art forms that deepen your connection with your newly discovered extraterrestrial acquaintances. If you do so, you will find that these galactically inspired materials are treasure chests full of gemlike messages of hope, Love, and Light.

Adonai.

On Science

Palpae

Read slowly through these messages. Galactically inspired essays hang heavily ripe, like bunches of grain dangling from fertile wheat stalks. They are fruitful with encouragement for you to develop a greater appreciation of your higher Self's purpose. To fulfill your Soul's primary purpose is the reason your spirit chose to incarnate in human form in these momentous, evolutionary times. Contemplate Self as a glorious beam of light. Remember, you are an essential, microcosmic flame of the universe. You are Soul forged from the passionate fires of Divine Creator's holy furnace.

Primordial wisdom, carefully tended by remnants of the ancients, has begun to quietly escape from chasms where much of the present generation would prefer to leave it buried and forgotten. Seemingly quiescent, its golden energies are gathering like clouds upon a horizon. Gently its whispers billow and shift, to Earth Mother's growing delight. Its powerful yet hushed voice is warning you of the dangerous ramifications of "modern-day" scientific methods and experiments, particularly in the fields of nuclear energy, nuclear weapons, chemical warfare, and genetic manipulation.

Logical individuals who are steeped in third-dimensional science hold a tight grip upon the mentality of the majority. It has become the norm for most scientists to completely exclude vast amounts of knowledge that are the spiritual treasures of mystically oriented people. They are also unable to project otherworld images before their inner sight as do practitioners of intuitive thought.

Many experts will no doubt take exception to the audacity of extraterrestrials who comment unfavorably upon a methodology based upon the careful collecting and screening of all data. Though it is certainly true that great strides have been made in electronic technology, physics, biology, and so forth, the scientific community has greatly compounded humanity's problems by failing to recognize that humans are spirits encased in physical forms and by routinely scoffing at intuitive individuals who indulge in "vaporous, unproductive, imaginary thought." Be that as it may; we reiterate that spiritually maturing humans are learning to stimulate their curious brain-minds by merging clear, logical thought with exquisite intuitive thought as it arises from their heart-minds.

Though humans engage in vastly divergent activities and much energy is expressed in their insatiable quest for knowledge, most scientific investigators fall quite short in incorporating the simple elements of spiritual law into their encyclopedia of formulae. Truth emanating as Creator's divine omniscient, energetic omnipresence *is law.* Universal Love manifesting as light *is law.* Intelligent essence of light in Beingness as the foundation of all matter *is law.*

Though the elements of Universal Law are simply constructed, your leaders routinely dispense with cosmic law; they only barely succeed in maintaining the majority in a perpetual state of confusion. Scientists obsessed with gathering facts for the sake of gathering facts leave little room for indulging in life-enhancing forms of imagining. Seldom, if ever, do they imagine themselves as multidimensional beings created from Love-Light substance, for they are unaware that life's vibrancy is built upon naturally occurring etheric elements. Nor do they think of themselves as spiritual light resembling a stack of fluffy pancakes. It would never occur to them that the physical body is like a bogged-down pancake resting at the bottom of a successively lighter pile of pancakes. They would be amazed to learn that the highest Self is perched on top of this remarkable pile, the unencumbered ultimate wonder, the shimmering radiance that is the glorious Soul.

Traditional, intellectual humans who repress any powerful energy that threatens to escape from their emotional bodies may do well to warm their bones from time to time with a dose of intuitive warmth. They may also assume a more open-minded approach toward the heritage and teachings that sustain spiritual people.

Humans who separate the cold calculations of their logical minds from the warm impressions of their intuitive minds have taken leave of their own hearts. Fear-filled dilemmas are constant reminders to the ego-indulging lower self that the higher Self is attempting to gain its attention. The higher Self, Soul, is constantly urging the lower self (brain-mind) to use telepathically channeled instructions the high Self relays through the subconscious (intuitive) mind.

Under conditions set forth in the contract that governs the beings of light of your universe, humans must increase the extremely low mental amperage to receive telepathic transmissions. To aid all humans to attain some degree of conscious awareness before history's final phase overtakes them, we will connect all who desire conscious linkage to the telepathic input of their spirit guides.

The road to the future is clearly marked. Ever ignorant of their true destiny, the majority stride down life's short highway attempting to ignore their Souls' urgent summons.

Perhaps you are one who would be pleased to participate in spiritual matters; perhaps you are not. Either way, it is our pleasurable task to serve all who ask. From our vantage point, we shine serene thought toward you. If you invite us in, you will find that thought exchange with your long-anticipated family from the stars is much more pleasurable than the persistent fears and worries that lurk in the depths of your indecisive minds.

To begin is to imply that something must also end; so, then, does this transmission.

Unconditional Love

Palpae

To practice unconditional Love is to approach and treat all other beings (animals and plants included) as you would an angel who has assumed physical form.

From time immemorial, higher worlds interjected certain specifications to emotionally sustain the beings who would eventually populate your planet, in particular, late-evolving humans. We may safely acknowledge that what was originally intended became seriously misconstrued. Therefore, Divine Intervention established unconditional Love around Earth as a powerful protective coating that would prevent unprepared beings from attaining the star grids. You may correctly interpret this to mean that a force field of Divine Energy enshrines Earth. Seen from your narrower perspective of galactic events, you may think that unconditional Love threatens you. However, honestly observing human affairs should enable you to reach the conclusion that the Spiritual Hierarchy's motives are for your highest good.

Unconditional Love—Divine Energy—is a precursor for intelligent life. Humanity's primary concern should be to integrate unconditional Love in all its activities and release Love's essence in such a way as to create upon Earth a microcosmic reflection of the macrocosm. For example, creating children is meant to be an ecstatic exchange of Love's reflection that draws men and women together, a mirror image of Omnipresent Creator's powerful love for Its creation. The difficulty has been that as humans developed intelligence, using the Law of Free Will they overstepped that which grants them the right to decide planetary matters.

To oppose unconditional Love is to permit judgment, intolerance, possessiveness, jealousy, hypocrisy, and fear to overwhelm you. To practice unconditional Love is to focus all desire toward serving the greater good of all beings through loving, compassionate understanding. Unconditional Love perceives from the other's viewpoint. It practices discernment so precisely that it becomes next to impossible to intentionally overstep another's will. One knows beyond a shadow of a doubt that nothing is between individuals and that everything is between the individual and God.

Beware these days, for warlike situations common to humans who play havoc with their free will have escalated into an alarming stockpile of nuclear armaments. Although this situation is somewhat reminiscent of the technology in place before the destruction of the Atlantean Empire, it is much more widespread. The Atlanteans remained in communication with the star councils and were aware of their place in the greater cosmos, but you are not. Thus, the state of your affairs is critical.

Unconditional Love will be your saving grace, which will ultimately prevent you from destroying Earth. Grace is cosmic energy the angelic realms disperse upon individuals who routinely request God's assistance. Grace is to be held in the fluttering wings of angels—a divine expression of unconditional Love.

Do not presume to ask us how to love. It is not such a difficult thing to do, and you are well versed in its nuances. Your problem is that your desire to bury yourselves in an accumulation of goods and ownership of others has overcome your good sense. To love is to be wise, to be of good will, to be of cheer, to express joy for the miracle of life. And to escape Earth's protective field of Divine Energy and return to the stars, you must learn to practice unconditional Love at all times and for all things. Your last lesson, Earth graduates, is to learn that unconditional Love bestows Oneness of Mind, which is the dwelling place of all spiritually advanced beings.

Divine Personalities

The Arcturians

The Christed Energy is the integrated, refined multidimensional resonation in being that emanates directly from Source Creator. To aid your understanding, which is overlaid with centuries of religious abuse and intolerance, the word *Sananda* has been adopted by the Regency star council to set the thought form "blissful ecstasy emanations of the Sun-Son" upon Earth to enlighten and accelerate human transformation. Those who are stuck in word energies that "push their buttons" are not easy with identities such as Jesus the Christ, Siddhartha Gautama Buddha, Mohammed, Krishna, Brahma, and so forth. The word *Sananda* radiates peace and unconditional, compassionate Love. It signifies the radiant presence of a being that is simultaneously identifiable, personal, and immediately available. Patricia's early manuscripts will use *Sananda* as the vast inexplicable energy of the Sun-Son. Later volumes will use Christ Essence, Christed One, and Buddha-Christ (East-West Oneness).

Because of human propensity to identify with individuals rather than with cosmic teachings, the device of giving the Christed Energy identity as a physical being is done as a tool to enhance enlightenment in slower awakening humans. Christed Essence is a universal vibration emanating from levels of energy so refined that it is inexplicable in human spiritual terms. Humans have seldom attained divine bliss, ecstatic joy, enlightened Soul development. Among those who have ascended into the thresholds of the highest vibratory essences of the Christed Ones are ascended masters, Jesus, Siddhartha, and Babaji (currently maintaining his one-thousand-year-old physical body in India).

We suggest that less attention be given to personalities inhabited by Divine Energy upon the gross physical planes and considerable more attention be given to Divine Truth as knowledge in action. Humans have an overriding tendency to miss the point. This is excusable considering their limited perception of universal harmonics.

PART IV: INTRODUCTION TO MALANTOR

The Song of Malantor

Tranquility is the savior.

Tranquility is the lodge house of the survivors.

Tranquility is the norm of God's Creation.

Tranquility is a state of being worth striving for.

May tranquility fill your loins, may your bones fill with tranquility's vibrant essence. May blessed peace illuminate the contours of your entire body.

May tranquility's perfumed aromas fill the passages of your mind. May your nostrils flare as tranquility's sweet bouquet stimulates your desire, your appetite for God.

Be bold in your spiritual search. Be an adventurer seeking immortal truths. Do not let the wayward glances of others distract you from your Soul's path.

Is there any other delight worth pursuing?

Can any essence fill one to overflowing as do the magnificent robes of God's Creation?

May none other come before you!

Fly as innocently as a bluebird winging into the ecstasy of the future. For it will come to pass that all sorrow will evaporate from the lands of Earth as if a great fog lifted from before your eyes.

Dream the Ageless Dream

Whispered renditions of ancient Memories too wonderful to die remain alive in your dreaming minds, their refrains resonating forever down time's fuzzy corridors. These remnants of human folklore were passed from generation to generation by bards who recorded their essences in poetry and song. Typical of these tales is the magical saga of Merlin, Arthur, Lancelot, and the valiant knights and mystical, beautiful women of Camelot. Like a splash of bright colors captured in a jar, Soul Memories of Camelot long buried in English bogs continue to arc their way through Earth's skies like a rainbow on a stormy day.

Why does this Memory retain its vibrancy? Because Camelot is a poignant reminder of one of humanity's finest hours. Refusing to evaporate, persisting through the dismal ages that followed, Arthur's vision of a fairer, more perfect world remains a dream that stimulates the emotional appetites of today's people. Those who persist in fantasizing a land whose king strove for personal and spiritual perfection are often lit with inner fires that inspire them to live as well as did the brave souls of Camelot.

Brave King Arthur was not content to rule by statutes that separated people from the Law of One. He ruled Camelot, a land where purity was honored above all things, where an act of chivalry was commonplace, where peace was superior to war, where inhabitants did not stumble from practicing cosmic teachings when adversity overcame them, where an empire was based upon Universal Law. And so, from out of the mists of time, the legend of Camelot rises like a Phoenix to spread its radiant wings over today's people, to settle comfort and hope upon the dreamers who persist in envisioning a world of perpetual harmony.

Though they are almost forgotten, allegorical tales from all over the world whisper of Cinnabar, Shambhala, and other magical places. Their delicious Memories continue to tease your imaginations with their exquisite flavors. Dazzling, mysterious images of men, women, and children whose bones turned to dust a very long time ago forever dwell in the fertile minds of those who remain young at heart.

A crystalline box containing diamonds of infinite possibilities was a gift the angels were instructed to prepare as God's offering to the budding human species as it took form upon its new planet—rich, verdant Earth. Entranced with the new environment, after a time the neonate species began to lose interest in the simple joys of youthful innocence. Eventually, many wayward newborns began to feel inadequate before God's perfection, and they lost patience with the details of cosmically inspired wisdom extraworld travelers had positioned around Earth to guide them. Bypassing the subtle tones of higher-world teachings, they became thoroughly captivated by Dark Lords. As humans' less-than-attentive eyes focused upon negative energies, the majority accepted interminable war and its aftereffects as the norm.

Camelot! A beautiful dream, a dream of utopia. Though the heart-minds of the majority retain cellular Memories of luscious Camelot, its reality has drifted into the mists of antiquity. Only a tantalizing fragrance remains to haunt the images that float through most humans' innermost thoughts—as if clouds of smoke drifting through the cracks of time's doorways were summoning them.

Though gauzy these wondrous Memories may be, even the most stubbornly resistant cannot completely escape them. The young at heart keep them ever so close. Flimsy images of mystical cities live eternally in the collective memory. Even those who retain only vague recall see a hint of shape whenever they succumb to the glow of a setting sun. Golden and jewel-studded, the colors and forms of mysterious places waver elusively through their minds.

Say then, are the magical cities impossible to duplicate? Only if you believe them to be. In reality they are not. The bright-hued radiance of Arcturus's crystalline buildings and the Pleiadian worlds' floating castlelike structures are reflected in dreamy visions that sleep in your hearts' Memories.

Say then, are the planets of Sirius and Antares and the galaxy Andromeda more blessed than the planets of Sol?

Not so! God grants equal opportunities as a constant for the many beings who inhabit the universes.

Observe Earth closely, if you will. Take careful note of her rocks, water, air, and multitudes of diverse plants and animals. Sadly, in a rather haphazard fashion humans created a situation that separates their lower selves from the venerable regions of their higher Selves. The tragic result is the torn fabric of "modern" industrialized society.

Long ago, as a developing but cosmically unsophisticated species, humans became entranced with that dire creature, fear, and its closest relatives—hate, anger, greed, jealousy, and mistrust—and invited them to establish permanent residence. Succumbing to the manipulations of these creatures, humans began to mold themselves into a potpourri of nations using confusing languages. Thus, they ignored the most basic of all sacred instructions: the practice of Universal Oneness, Love-Light. Even at their best, it became impossible for them to foster anything other than ambiguous, uncertain relationships. Paradoxically, the people who prefer to call themselves *man*—excluding by inference that who is wo-man—maintain an innate capacity to execute Love's powerful energy, though they have forgotten that God-Oneness is not capable of division. Most view That Which Is Omnipotent as a fractionated entity.

It is our purpose to devise formulae for the promotion of goodwill among humans. We are beings who have structured our worlds solely in alignment with the tenets of the Law of One, that which radiates Light-Love. As such, we have received Omnipotent Creator's permission to travel the stars. Energies that maintain the space grids in harmonious motion are ours to freely access. However, we did not achieve a state of permanent bliss without a struggle to attain spiritual perfection.

A curious species, humans. They push relentlessly to open the elusive doors behind which mysteries that their immaturity has long denied them are stored. Yet the challenge of potential discovery is too tantalizing to ignore.

As you move into a state of greater cosmic awareness, you will receive an engraved invitation to join your starry family in partaking of a grand celestial banquet. Nonexclusive, our guest list potentially includes the entire range and scope of tumultuous beings who inhabit Earth. Delightful dishes will be extracted directly from enticing fruits that heretofore only dreamers and mystics dared taste. The selection will be so magnificent it will be sure to tempt the palate of the most discriminating diner. Before your wondering eyes huge platters heaped with steaming stars will pass, a sumptuous entrée deliciously yours.

Prior to joining us in the great stellar hall, however, you must establish a comfortable acquaintance with your hosts, beings of light who hail from far-distant suns. In our eagerness, representatives from distant galaxies and more than one universe have gathered to greet you.

I, Malantor of Arcturus, was a human on ancient Earth. I remember her well. Her people I have not forgotten. Now here I come like a beam of sunlight along the flower-hued, humming hallways of a starship that hails from (seemingly) far-distant Arcturus. Ecstasy! I yearn to intertwine as one energy field with my human family, whom I so grandly love. Yes, I experience Oneness with my sister Patricia as well. That which is Malantor-Patricia project a single field of unified telepathic energy. Though our individual essences remain intact, we are simultaneously capable of experiencing Oneness in all areas of our being, as are you also with us, human family. If your brittle egos would but allow it, you would come to understand what an expansive being you-we truly are.

Expanded View of Eagles of the New Dawn

This day, as is every day, is particularly precious. The heavy vibrational tones that hold Earth captive in her third-dimensional slot are rapidly refining. Time's patterns are being cleansed of all superfluous residue. The glorified moment of her octaval transformation nears.

To revamp the vibratory refinement of a planet's entire cellular structure requires a commitment by a multitude of beings. Earth's Spiritual Hierarchy, collaborating in harmonious Oneness with light-resonating extraterrestrials of the greater galactic community, remains constantly alert to every subtle sigh Earth issues. Awakening human starseeds are increasingly aware of the vital role they play in the process of aligning Earth with the magnified stellar regions. To facilitate every nuance of energy necessary for Earth's celestial realignment, all ascension-motivated humans must cooperatively interact and hold light within their geographic time zones by practicing group and individual Earth-healing meditations.

Understand that a great many species that make up Earth's inhabitants did not originate within the primal clouds from which Earth was formed. The vibrations of many humans, animals, plants, precious metals, and gemstones are specific to other planets within this solar family and other star systems: Venus, Mars, Arcturus, Pleiades, Antares, Deneb, Orion, and Sirius, to name a few. Millions of these multiform extraterrestrials surrendered to deep cosmic sleep and repetitive birth-death cycling to enrich their Souls. As these starseeds were laid upon Earth and became subject to the physical laws that maintain heavy gravitational worlds, they were encased in a variety of physical "suits."

The foregoing would appear to imply that starseeds took over other beings' bodies. However, it is not necessary for starseeds to merge with the physical or emotional bodies of others. Many human starseeds have a mirror image living more or less geographically opposite them on Earth.

We do not wish to alarm you. Our intent is to broaden your scientific and historical knowledge. Starseed Souls are not unlike other Souls who originally settled on Earth in that they, too, are trapped in multiple life recycling commonplace to this planet. Many lifetimes ago, the vast majority of them lost awareness of their extrasolar origins and the reasons they became caught in Earth's illusive karmic webs.

Starseeds often refer to themselves as wanderers. To them, it seems as if they are forever attempting to grasp a greater insight into an indefinable, intangible something that appears to be hovering next to them—unseen, unspoken, silent. Inexplicable loneliness and a deep-felt hunger for

Home permeates their wounded hearts. No matter how much energy they expend in complying with society's rules, they never quite manage to comfortably integrate themselves into the norm. They have immense difficulty trying to belong. They often suffer chronic allergies, headaches, ringing ears, back problems, and other forms of physical distress. Some, especially sensitive individuals, are prone to chronic depression, bipolar disease, and schizophrenia. They feel that city environments, other people, and technological advances seem oddly out of sync, outmoded, unfamiliar. A sense of "What am I doing here?" is not uncommon.

As their Soul Memories are reactivated by the escalating cosmic energies they are absorbing, this generation's starseeds are overcome with an intense desire to awaken. Few are permanently satisfied with any life situation. They yearn to move ahead. Caught in the momentum, they keep moving from place to place, relationship to relationship, job to job, city to city, state to state, country to country. Like yo-yos they feel pulled backward and forward, up and down. They experience linear time and spatial reality as slippery substances that resemble mercury flowing from a crushed thermometer, something that cannot be grasped or held. In social and work situations they are moving into positions that best serve their specialized stellar abilities, talents, and resources. Often with a great deal of personal struggle and sacrifice, they are extricating themselves from unfulfilling relationships and other situations.

Though they may have no recall, their karmic circumstances and starry origins are magnetic forces attracting Soul-related starseeds to one another as evidenced by emotional triggers that both attract and repel them. They are drawn into groups who instinctively recognize that a familial bond connects them. Their guides assist them by "arranging" a variety of encounters and opportunities.

Most starseeds have grown inordinately fond of their adopted planet, Earth. They have developed a deep, passionate love for this jewellike world, which appears to be in its death throes. They are obsessed with activating their lives' highest purpose in order to serve and heal her. Their intense desire to fulfill their destinies is an awakening summons, a bell urging them to vibrantly manifest their Souls' radiant song.

All self-activating humans (starseeds and otherwise) are valiant beings. It is inordinately unusual for humans to willing subject themselves to all kinds of discomfort and sacrifice to achieve a highly envisioned goal. Starship personnel call those who are committed to achieving light-body ascension in this lifetime their worthy assistants, indomitable ones, eagles of the new dawn. Their eagerness to serve Prime Creator through self-healing acts, thereby establishing a system of light-enhanced energy upon the planetary grids, is elevating Earth's vibration and is thrusting her body into a higher vibrational realm. Their passionate attention to the details of spiritual enlightenment is laying to rest the final years of unevolved human history.

Beings of light from rosy red Arcturus have pledged themselves to the starseeds who request assistance. No matter the star system for which you feel an affiliation, you are urged to fine-tune yourselves for a pending intergalactic gathering presently scheduled to take place in Earth year 2012.

All telepathed writings currently being released substantially widen humanity's perspective of the multisystem-multidimensional dynamics of the universe. Those who freely indulge in the growing bounty of metaphysical literature are absorbing massive portions of love, hope, joy, courage, faith, and trust. Those adventurous beings, in the face of a seemingly contradictory feeling that humanity is frantically succumbing to the dark side, are fast coming to the realization that these are exceedingly sacred and transformative times.

Our goal is to assist you in developing a healthy, loving attitude and respect for one another and for Earth. To help you achieve a broader understanding of humanity's responsibility to protect and nurture the plants and animals with whom you share planetary space, we are supplying you with spiritual tools to realign and synchronize your harmonic resonations with those of your vibrationally refining planet.

The growing obligation starseeds feel to serve their higher Selves is very unusual, from a historical perspective. Within the confines of a technology-structured, war-oriented, religiously dogmatic society, the drive to spiritually hone oneself is deemed irresponsible, dysfunctional behavior. Patricia is a prime example of our meaning. Her natural talent is to receive and transmit multidimensional thought waves. Because of her passionate desire to spiritually fulfill herself through service to endangered wolves, she earned the star title Manitu (spirit keeper). Now her challenge is to constantly maintain herself in a state of readiness for thought-alignment with the Arcturians, the star councils, and other beings of light—not an occupation deemed worthy or sane by the human majority.

When natural transdimensional telepaths keep themselves in alignment with flows of refined stellar energies, copious amounts of Love-Light filter through their bodies and pour onto the planetary grids. As Manitu-assigned starseeds concentrate their attention upon an animal or plant—both individual and species—a pulsating, radiant beam of Love moves through the ground into their root chakras and exits their crown chakras, establishing a grid of connective light between Earth and fifth- and sixth-dimensional starships. Their auric bodies begin to accelerate high-wattage light. Sustained energy of this caliber creates a powerful vortex surge onto the planetary grids and creates a permanent coupling among Earth, humans, and transdimensional starships. Whenever thought-linkage is achieved between humans and animals or plants, the many become One. Then, if for only a moment, a state of divinely inspired creative resonation is activated.

The production of this essay has been a joint endeavor of Malantor of Arcturus and Patricia of Earth, instructional format in accord with high resonations of the Office of the Christ. We are mutually grateful to you for affording us an opportunity to converse with you through the medium of the written word. With utmost regard for your struggles, we encourage you to persevere in thought, word, and deed to uplift and encourage yourself and others to maintain a spiritual focus throughout these dangerous yet transformative years.

Part V: Childhood's End

A Challenge to Love, Childhood's End, Galactic Contract

Palpae for the Arcturians

Many of you ride waves of temperament fluctuations whenever you contemplate Earth's accelerating deterioration. If you routinely suffer from extreme emotional, mental, or physical duress in these evolutionary times, it is important for you to establish lasting contact with Divine Intelligence.

Beloved beings, be courageous. Be solid and firm when confronted with life's growing challenges. Within you is a reservoir of untapped strength. Do not hesitate to create innovative ways to explore the rich worlds that lie within your inner Selves. Be discerning in your choice of associates and activities in which you participate. Strive for harmonious agreement between your awakening sense of burgeoning spirituality and your worldly responsibilities. When plagued with feelings of unworthiness or self-doubt, give your busy minds opportunities to spend more time in inward reflection. As you dive deeper and deeper into meditative silence, eventually you will learn to consciously communicate with beings of light.

Routinely and enthusiastically state your intention for emotional, mental, physical, and spiritual healing and growth. Attending to your spiritual needs will greatly aid your ethereal guides to incorporate finer degrees of light filaments (additional DNA helix) into your cellular matrices. This is best accomplished when you are in a meditative mode.

We proclaim! The foregoing is the primary spiritual task of all who are preparing themselves for light-body ascension and the only feasible course for seekers of infinite wisdom to pursue.

The Spiritual Hierarchy is laying a clearly marked path for you to follow, a way out of the perplexing maze of torment and struggle characteristic of most lives. Spiritual councilors and instructional materials are becoming widely available, but you must seek them out and, with discernment, practice their teachings.

It is almost impossible to explain to you the higher-world dynamics set into motion whenever a human states an intention to take the first faltering step upon the spiritual path. As your ethereal guides, we are not unaware of the rocky road you must travel. It is difficult for humans to understand that Earth's plants and animals are less cumbersomely wrapped in spiritual somnolence than they are and do not suffer so from mental and emotional Soul fatigue.

Clouds hang majestically suspended above Earth. Eternally seeking perfection of form, they easily adapt themselves to their fluctuating environment—the rhythms of wind, heat, Earth, moon, and sun. Like clouds, spiritually adept humans are learning to gently flow with the currents of rhythmic energies that pull at Earth as she moves into transdimensional transport position.

In 1987, Earth entered the first phase of a space-time corridor that empties upon the Plains of Perpetual Resonation. Since that transformative year, humans who stay closely tuned to nature's rhythms have begun to form a distinct impression that soft, angelic wings are constantly fluttering around them. Many are becoming aware of the whispered tones that indicate a celestially inspired communique. They are becoming quite proficient at accessing multilevel telepathic directives from their ethereal guides on a moment-to-moment basis, and they have come to realize that there is no need to perform elaborate ceremonies to call upon the angels.

The only effective method for establishing internal serenity is through daily meditation practice. It is next to impossible for your active human minds to glean information from the still streams of the subconscious and superconscious if you do not take time to experience silence. Telepathic thought floats upon subtle waves of energy. To quiet inward turbulence, learn to relax and follow your breath as you gently inhale and exhale.

One of the greatest challenges facing you as you begin to communicate transdimensionally is to learn to distinguish Love-Lights's melodic refrains from the heavier tones of entities who lie in wait for the spiritually unwary.

As you venture inward, passionately and clearly state your intention to be in Oneness with principles of Divine Light. Entities who inhabit lower astral levels are attracted to those who fail to set well-defined light boundaries. Remember, Love-Light is easily called. Protection is immediately available when you call upon the angelic regions to sustain you in perfect harmonious pitch.

When communicating with other humans, plants, and animals, always speak in a well-modulated voice. Generously dispense Love's high energy all around you. A friendly smiling face is a magnificent portrait for all the world to see. Emulate the Christ Essence—Sananda—and other members of the Holy Seraphim and various brotherhoods of light (including the Intergalactic Brotherhood of Light), who never transmit negative-based energies that would result in mental, emotional, physical, or spiritual harm to other beings.

Be wise and stay alert. Beings who speak to you from the light realms are as easy to recognize as the beloved faces of your families and friends. Essences of Light never waver in form when challenged to identify themselves. Energies that serve Light fill your emotional bodies with sensations of ecstasy and unrestricted Love. They caress you with melodious song as if you were resting in a magnificent garden of singing flowers. Telepathic interchange with light-bodied beings is like listening to the angelic strums of lutes and harps radiating from heaven's majestic cathedral. Their thoughts are as sweetly scented as a rose. When you invite energies of Light to be as One with you, they are immediately present.

Commit to live in a sacred manner, that is, from a place of high integrity. Resolve to be one with those who travel the golden road. Critical to your growing awareness is knowing that those who refuse to serve Light and fail to recognize the Law of Love place themselves in jeopardy of abduction by manipulative entities. Like clowns pretending to laugh at folly, they put themselves in peril of tarnishing their spirit bodies' brilliance.

Truly, only the spiritually lonely choose to live with their faces turned from Divine Source, where they will never learn to recognize Love's radiant features.

We, the Arcturian contingency of the Intergalactic Brotherhood of Light, are in service to humanity's evolution into the realms of light. If we do no more than guide a few to a greater recognition of Love-Light, we will serve our own higher calling, for to retrieve even one precious jewellike Soul for God is a worthy endeavor. Our forms are of light and to disperse absolute Love-Light among you is our primary goal.

The intergalactic starfleet comprises a body of integrated Souls of multisystem origin. Joined in mutual Oneness, our intention is to perpetually serve Divine Perfection. Individuals serving aboard fifth- and sixth-dimensional starships are making themselves known to humans who are openly receptive to honing their multilevel telepathic skills. These delightful humans understand the purpose of our mission and know that Earth faces no threat of extraterrestrial invasion from the light domains.

Do not set aside these essays as foolish nonsense. Find the wherewithal to thoughtfully study them, or search diligently for truth in a more appealing fashion. Delay nary a moment in your endeavor to seek Love-Light's essence, for Earth time is fast drawing to a close. If you have been a seeker of spiritual knowledge for many years, do not allow yourself to stagnate under the supposition that you have mastered all life's lessons.

Set aside a moment to take a brief inward journey through humanity's past. Complete your travels by offsetting any painful images that arise with a perfected vision of a glorious, peaceful future. What you see is reserved not only for Earth's evolution but for the entire galaxy and beyond. Know that the entire universe and all it contains is moving toward an expanded appreciation of vibrational light.

Humans who choose not to evolve during this lifetime and refuse to accept the challenges of spiritual responsibility will not soon travel as our companions upon the starships. Fear not for the demise of their Souls, however, for Soul energy is not something that can be destroyed. The Creator provided Soul with unlimited dimensions of experience. Indeed, the number of universes and octave levels within the universes would astound you, as would the number of stars and inhabited planets in this galaxy alone. Timeless, eternal Soul has unlimited opportunities and unlimited choices. Souls in human form who choose to honor the forces of negativity will simply settle at levels that are appropriate to their light vibrations.

Healing modifications within your solar system will continue to accelerate until a moment of supreme energy is reached, which will facilitate transfer to a state of refined light. Humans who are particularly spiritually alert have long been aware that Earth is reaching the point of graduation. For many years they have been quietly gathering around the planet to play active roles in this magnificent adventure.

Your true mother is Earth. Throughout the short span of time humans have lived upon her, she has borne their tortures, their aggressions, and the many ways in which they mutilate themselves and other creatures. It may surprise you to learn that your Mother is quite aware of those who truly love her and with tender warmth nurture and care for her needs.

The following will illustrate the power your thoughts have to facilitate Earth's healing: In February 1988, a world group meditation focused thought upon Australia's majestic Ayer's Rock. A mound of regal energy, Ayer's Rock sits upon a grid vortex and has always been highly sacred to the aborigines. At a prearranged time, a laserlike beam of thought was aimed at Ayer's, which it gratefully absorbed. This event was extremely successful in releasing stress that accumulates within the southern tectonic plates as Australia mourns the massive loss of plant and animal life in the rain forests of her sister continents, Africa and South America.

People who consider themselves experts in geology, biology, physics, mathematics, chemistry, and so forth have gathered much data that are technically correct. We grant them that. Nevertheless, we continue to point out that current standards fail to consider the pleading hums that issue from Earth's crust. The scientific community has yet to discern that melodious vibration is the base energy of all "inert" matter. We state again: All things in the manifest universe are formed from components of Divine Omniscient Love-Light.

Eventually, all of you will approach Earth's creatures from a holistic attitude. Then you will willingly shoulder your responsibilities as guardians and will exhibit unconditional Love for all life forms.

It is long past time for industrialized nations to adapt ways that are in agreement with Universal Law. Nevertheless, many of you have already begun to fine-tune your intuitive ears to Earth's vibrations and are becoming telepathically connected to the intricate solar web that allows you to communicate multidimensionally. You are approaching sacred teachings with greater understanding and are becoming comfortable with cosmic knowledge. Now it is not so difficult to accept all matter as an expression of Creator's Love-Light Essence.

You are as delightful as children, and you can be just as exasperating. On the surface it would appear that most of you prefer to satiate one fleeting physical and emotional impulse after another rather than shoulder the hardy tasks that result in spiritual maturity. There you sit, the appealing allure of transitory pleasure dripping from your tongues like ice cream on a summer's day.

Quite soon you will find yourselves immersed in extremely difficult times. Explosive energies are rapidly accumulating within the planet body and in human society. Unless you have mastered the use of effective spiritual tools, you will not be able to escape the impact of suppressed power when it bursts forth.

Both positive- and negative-oriented extraterrestrials use your entertainment and informational devices to put across their messages. Society abounds with movies, books, music, and art whose subtle and not-so-subtle extraworld origins escape notice. These methods are used by forces of light to assist those who are opting for light ascension as well as by forces of evil who lie in wait for the unwary. Humans, you must make a heroic effort to vibrationally advance before Dark Lords capture your inattentive spirits. We advise you to form a more discerning comprehension of the things you focus your attention upon.

Those who acknowledge and welcome beings of light will be much more motivated to put away their destructive weapons, their feeble attempts to manipulate nature to suit their will, and the illusion of many nations ruled by pseudopowerful military, political, economic, and religious figures. Such mundane things do not entrance beings who understand and practice unconditional Love.

Many unattended household chores have accumulated throughout your species' short stay on Earth. Because of centuries of procrastination, a multitude of urgent, backbending tasks awaits you. You have much to do! You have outgrown the option to rampage freely about your planetary playpen in a state of perpetual immaturity. The time has come to store your childish toys, to permanently lock the doors upon your tortured past. Mature beings express attitudes of compassionate Love. The long summer of adolescence is played out. It is time for you to enter the cosmic classroom with your pencils sharpened and your faces scrubbed.

All humans are invited to the stars. However, those who choose nonparticipation in spiritual matters will remain stuck in birth-death recycling. As such, their spirits will be relocated to a dimensional environment that resonates low-wattage light. Eventually, those tormented beings will honor their Souls' natural instinct for light, and they will reactivate their search for God.

As you spiritually mature you will resume the wonderful delights of your once-childlike innocence. An aware adult-child knows its proper place in the universe and vigorously embraces that which must be accomplished in an attitude of service without temperamental displays. Joyous, spontaneous laughter comes naturally to mature beings who listen to the intuitive whispers that radiate from their heart-minds. Remembering childhood's innocence, a truly mature entity is fully cognizant that a polliwog swimming lazily in a summer pool is a magical display of integrated Divine Love in perpetual agreement with Prime Creator.

Reflect upon the nation that rather euphemistically refers to itself as the "United" States. Inwardly, create an image of the sacred document in which the founding fathers wrote, "All men are created equal." Does this statement not imply that they understood all of you are One? It would be exceedingly grand if all humans were to immediately cease their manipulative behaviors and prejudicial attitudes toward others. The Law of Cause and Effect stipulates that whatever is done to another is also done to self. It would be good to expand your narrow concept of "others" to include all life forms: all creatures who inhabit Earth and those into the far reaches of the galaxy. The uniqueness that qualifies an individual as a distinct being within the One is not born from "better than" or "lesser than" qualities but from choices made by the Soul on its evolutionary journey.

We return to the subject of telepathy as a universally understood language. It is our purpose to outline details of telepathic thought that allow for no degree of misinterpretation. However, remember that solar language adapted to written or oral language can often produce awkwardly phrased statements.

Earth is a planet of confusion and chaos. Much conflict and turmoil is directly related to the limited range of your communication skills. Misunderstanding permeates everything you think, say, and do. As your evolution to light progresses, clarity of telepathic communication will become commonplace and will completely supersede compartmentalized, subject-oriented speech.

Comparing voice communication with the benefits of mind communication is like contrasting a Model T Ford with a sports car. In time, you will gain a greater appreciation of the extent to which spoken language has delayed your growth and hampered your freedom to move in and out of alternative realities.

Your communication handicaps arise from the energy polarities that permeate your multiple societies to the point that you are essentially incapable of comprehending the inner beings of your family and friends. To overcome these difficulties, you must make a concerted effort to master the telepathic process. Your first step is to understand that you are capable of dynamic interaction with all living things via the energies of thought exchange.

Times are rapidly changing. You are faced with many difficult lessons and you will be tested on many levels. There is a great deal waiting for you to assimilate. As you digest the teachings presented throughout this manuscript, we hope you will come to a clear realization that spiritual evolution is an actuality and is simply executed but that it also requires a great deal of determination and attention to detail.

The day rapidly approaches when the entire intergalactic fleet will gather our starships before your eyes. On that auspicious day, star council coordinators will join Earth's delegates in a precedent-setting session upon the command ship. (It may surprise you to learn that humans who have achieved spiritual master status have always acted as your intermediaries with the greater galactic community.) As the meeting convenes, the galactic contract—the requirements for humans to resume their rightful places as full cosmic citizens—will be stated for all Earth's governments and all Earth's people to clearly understand and agree to.

People who rule your most powerful nations and institutions have, for many years, been quite aware of our presence. Also, they have been apprised of all contractual stipulations for planetary ascension and for integrating awakened humanity into the star councils.

All committed starseeds are directed to focus energy upon Earth's principal energy grids, such as the pyramid of Giza, Machu Picchu, Stonehenge, Mayan and Aztec pyramids, Ayer's Rock, and the Burmuda and Lemurian triangles. The information that flows from their creative minds originates primarily in the United States, the British Isles, western Europe, and Australia. Communiques between the brotherhoods of light (including the Intergalactic Brotherhood) and the Spiritual Hierarchy are already in effect with cooperative humans who stay in telepathic contact with the star councils. Star-to-Earth communiques ring clear when processed through the minds of humans who live in nations where a certain, albeit extremely limited, tolerance for "paranormal" artistic expression is permitted. Rigidly constructed religious, economic, political, and military systems in vogue even in supposedly free countries can be intimidating to the psychically gifted.

We suggest that anyone who considers it a moral obligation to interfere with people dedicated to manifesting unconditional Love-Light observe the skies before undertaking any unkind act. All awakening starseeds (human or otherwise) are constantly monitored by the Spiritual Hierarchy and the brotherhoods of light. Be aware that everything you even consider doing that could violate another's free will is a major transgression of Universal Law.

Earth ark is about to dock in a perpetual Garden of Eden–like beauty. Harmonious existence will be the norm in the era of the new dawn. Delightful life and rapturous Love will be the common experience of all beings who choose to remain Soul-connected to majestically evolved Earth.

Scan the skies for the return of the Dove. It carries in Its beak a sprig of celestial holly—a branch of hope, peace, and Love—principal gifts to your forlorn world. Rejoice! Your anguish and pain are softly fading.

Children of Earth, never forget that you are cherished, protected, and dearly loved by your family from the stars.

Those who have journeyed this far into the manuscript should be aware by now that all it takes to communicate with us is an open and quiet mind. The telepathic process requires that you be willing to intimately integrate your ego personality with other minds. To begin, you must be constantly alert to and honor the resonating presence of your guides, for they stand ready to teach, assist, and counsel you.

Even a slight understanding as to who we are and why we have surrounded Earth with our starships will help to lessen the fear that threatens to strain humans' fragile stability. It certainly is not our intention to set anyone's heart palpitating in alarm.

To soften the shocking aspect of a sky filled with UFOs, we would have you welcome this event long before it occurs. This will settle you more quickly into what is, after all, only the norm. To extend your comfort zone prior to that awesome day, we recommend you make it a habit to closely watch the daytime sky for unusual cloud formations and the nighttime sky for brilliant flashes of green-red-gold-blue sparkles that twinkle in front of the stars. We also suggest you become familiar with and scrutinize all available data on the kinds of extraterrestrials who are in Earth residence.

Fear not those who come to you in Love-Light, for it is their intent to manifest peace and Universal Law.

Process these thoughts, Patricia, and settle them into your computer.

You who are wandering seekers will soon come into your own. Your driving motivation to permanently reactivate your Soul energies will aid your ascension into light-body form. In the era of the new dawn, evolved humanity's primary focus will be upon spiritual endeavors. The negativity that has tormented your world since the beginning of human history is to be replaced with radiant, colored lights floating to the ground from the skies of a refreshed Earth.

Search! Search through every hidden aspect of yourselves to root out every vestige of discomfort that lies within. Self-purification is essential if you wish to fully awaken. Cleanse your emotional, mental, and physical bodies. Sparkle and gleam until you shine like an early-morning meadow softened with dew. Love with compassion the reality of your entire being. Do not fear the complexities of your inner selves or the subtle ambiguities of your human condition. Honor and embrace your inner darkness and resolve to replace it with light. Do so in a quickened manner! Your good intentions and efforts will greatly help you move through the oppressive years in a fairly unencumbered manner.

Meditate upon each essay's nuances with an open and receptive mind. Give your beautiful heart-mind permission to dive deep into each one's sublime waters. As you become reborn in Love-Light's perfect innocence and as your vibrational level accordingly refines, you will become reacquainted with members of your extrastellar family. Our lives will intertwine as One. Together we will float upon the etheric cords of shimmering rainbow lights that bind planet to planet and sun to sun. Remember what it is you truly desire. Never again turn your back upon the golden road that is taking you Home.

We salute you from *Marigold–City of Lights*, which hovers high above the North American continent. Among us are many beings who once wandered in human form. Eventually, we rediscovered Creator's abundant treasures and the key that accesses the stars.

It is not necessary ever to feel that you are alone. Summon us to abide as One with you. Assimilate the truth of our mutual being, the truth of who we really are, the children of the stars.

We are not unaware that our messages may seem like the obscure tidings of a scattered reality. Nevertheless, as you integrate the simple beauty of their harmonious tones, you may discover that you have begun to calm the beating of your passionate hearts and still the calculations of your busy minds. As you do so, you will develop an inner peace and an expanded view of life's rich treasures. In time it will not be as difficult to comprehend that there has never been anything that really separated us. You will understand that you are special members of a great cosmic family, that in every sense you and we are truly One.

Beloved ones, we challenge you to express Love! We challenge you to radiate Light!

Energy amplitude completed. In an ecstatic display of Light-Love, we embrace all awakening humans and our precious starseeds.

Adonai.

Appendix

Glossary

Adonai: Hebrew for "Lord." Divine Energy associated with the word's vibration assures Patricia of her light-level telepathic connection.

Akashic Records: Cosmic journals that contain the records of the Soul's journey. These records are attended to by the angelic realms. With permission, Earth's spiritual masters and empowered enlightened beings are able to peruse them.

Ascended masters: Earth-incarnated souls who have overcome death, have assumed their bodies of light, and have attained God-realized Christ Consciousness.

Astral planes: Fourth dimension, planes of instant manifestation. The astral is where reincarnating souls attached to Earth dwell between lives. The astral planes are vast and multilayered. The lower astral is where negative beings and negative thought forms reside. The region referred to in religious texts as heaven is the upper astral. See *Octave*.

AUM, OHM: Prime tone, a basic ingredient of universal energy. See *Hum.*

BLUE CRYSTAL PLANET: Closest English translation for the principal light-bodied planet of the Arcturian star system. Primary planning and gathering planet for the multiuniversal, multidimensional star councils.

BRAIN-MIND: The logical mind where the computerlike calculations of the physical brain are stored. See *Conscious mind.*

BROTHERHOODS OF LIGHT: Brotherhood means *in Oneness.* There are many orders of brotherhoods of light. Earth's embodied and ascended masters are members of these brotherhoods. The Intergalactic Brotherhood of Light, which is made up of spiritually advanced extraterrestrials, is one order. Another important brotherhood associated with Earth's ascension is the Order of Melchizedek. The Office of the Christ heads the brotherhoods of light. *The Book of Knowledge: The Keys of Enoch* by J. J. Hurtak is an excellent resource for information on the brotherhoods. See "Suggested Books and Movies." See *Intergalactic Brotherhood of Light.*

CELESTIAL HOME: Also referred to as Central Sun. The Soul yearns to return to Celestial Home. It is the Soul's journey's end.

CELLULAR MATRICES: The molecular makeup of all third-dimensional physical matter. Used to describe the human body as well as Earth's body.

CHAKRA: Wheels of energy that make up the body's inner anatomy. Often described as lotus blossoms in Eastern tradition. Chakras are widely covered in Hindu,

Buddhist, and Yoga texts. Shirley MacLaine's "Inner Workout" video is an excellent study and meditation source for the Western mind.

CONSCIOUS MIND: Third-dimensional brain functions. Mental layers of linear-logical thought. Same as brain-mind.

DARK LORDS: Evil, manipulative, controlling beings who throughout history have attempted to hold humanity in their clutches. They are referred to as satanic beings, Lucifer, and the dark angels. See *Grays.*

DENSITY OCTAVE, DIMENSIONAL OCTAVE: See *Octave.*

EAGLES OF THE NEW DAWN: Awakened humans (and animals) who interact with the star councils to serve Earth's evolution. Also called sky warriors.

ENERGY FIELDS: Energy fields range from subtle to force-field magnitude. The energy field that surrounds the human body is the aura. See *Grids* and *Vortex.*

ETHERIC GRID STRANDS: See *Grids.*

FIFTH DIMENSION: Dimension of refined light. Arcturians are fifth- and sixth-dimensional beings. Negative beings are unable to penetrate into the realms of light substance.

FOURTH DIMENSION: See *Astral planes.*

GOD-REALIZED: An enlightened, evolved individual who has attained Christ Consciousness. Spiritual masters are God-realized.

GRACE: To receive grace is to be held in the fluttering arms of angels. Grace is an energy field that descends upon humans from Divine sources for physical, emotional, and mental healing, and to assist in fulfilling the Soul's life purpose.

Grays: Manipulative extraterrestrials who are in alliance with Dark Lords. The Grays are responsible for human abductions and cattle mutilations. See *Dark Lords.* See *Hidden Mysteries* by Joshua D. Stone and *UFOs and the Nature of Reality* from Ramtha for detailed information.

Grids, gridlines, space grids, star grids, strands: Crisscrossing webs of light, sound, color, and scent that make up Earth's spiritual body. Starships also travel upon grids of light that weave through space. Grids of light connect galaxy to galaxy, star to star, planet to planet, moon to moon, and so forth. Refer to Volume I, Part III for more detailed information.

Harmonic coordinates of the galactic hum: The sound coordinates of the grids. See *Hum.*

Heart-mind: The intuitive, spiritual mind. The heart chakra is the location of the heart-mind. It is where we connect with our higher Selves and our Soul Memories.

Hum: Cosmic creative vibration, the prime or God energy expressed as Aum (Amen) or Ohm. Matter's tonal qualities. Pythagoras described hum as the music of the spheres.

I Am: The Self's identity as Soul.

Intergalactic Brotherhood of Light: Spiritually evolved, light-formed, fifth- and sixth-dimensional extraterrestrials from many star systems and many universes. See *Spiritual Hierarchy* and *Star councils.*

Language of the Sun: Common mode of telepathic communication natural to all beings. Also called solar tongue or solar language.

Light-Love or Love-Light: Light is the first manifestation of God in form; Love is God's Essence or energy. Light-Love incorporates Creation's energy as a physical manifestation. Sound (vibration) is integral to Light-Love energy. Throughout the ages Earth's God-realized spiritual masters have referred to Light-Love as unconditional Love.

LIGHT STRANDS: See *Grids*.

LORDS OF DARKNESS: See *Dark Lords*.

LOVE AND LOVE: Unconditional Love is integrated Cosmic Intelligence. However, love is the emotion humans feel for others, their pets, and Earth.

MANITU: Meaning "spirit keeper," it is the title the Intergalactic Brotherhood bestows on people whose life's purpose is planetary healing.

MARIGOLD—CITY OF LIGHTS: Intergalactic Brotherhood Earth-based mother ship. Authors may refer to it by other names, perhaps *City of Lights, Jeweled City, Crystal City, New Jerusalem.* The term *Marigold* was given to this writer as a symbolic clue that cosmic light incorporates vibration, color, and scent. The mother ship in the movie *Close Encounters of the Third Kind* portrays her essence, though *Marigold–City of Lights* is much larger.

MEMORIES: Aspect of Self-knowledge slumbering humanity has forgotten; Soul Memories. As we awaken to our spiritual nature, the Memories are reactivated.

OCTAVE: A dimensional or density span. The vibrational layers within a dimension are not unlike the notes of the musical scale, ever softening in an upward or refining manner.

Psychic protection: The purposeful use of Light-Love when meditating or channeling. The following steps are recommended: cleansing one's physical environment with incense or sacred herbs (smudging); requesting Christ Consciousness energy (see *Spiritual Hierarchy*) to assist; visualizing light running through the chakras and surrounding the body in an energy bubble; using a repetitive, vibrational tone or mantra (for example, Aum or Ohm); and routinely forcefully challenging any entity with the statement "Are you of the Light (spiritual beings)?" (See Volume I, Part II, "Patricia Meets Palpae.") Beings of light expect to be challenged. Negative beings cannot penetrate the layers of a Light-Love established forcefield.

Resonant vibrational hum: Degree of refined light vibrating within a dimensional octave.

Sananda: The Christ, or High Christ Consciousness. Christ Essence. Higher vibrational identification given to Earth's Avatar Supreme by the Intergalactic Brotherhood of Light. Incarnated upon Earth as Jesus, Krishna, Buddha, Mohammed, Quetzalcoatl, and more. Masculine vibration.

Sixth dimension: See *Fifth dimension.*

Sky warriors: See *Eagles of the new dawn.*

Space grids: See *Grids.*

Space poppies: Refers to scented, flowered coordinates that are the by-products or the bouquets of the harmonics. The Arcturians find the symbolic use of flowers helpful in explaining the fragrant qualities of the light grids.

Space-time: In this text, refers to the linear structures of third-dimensional spatial and time realities as well as to the ebb and flow of fourth-dimensional space and time.

Spiritual Hierarchy: Body of One, supreme spiritual council in service to Earth's ascension. The central figure is the Christ Essence. The council includes archangels and angelic realms, ascended masters, the brotherhoods of light (including the Intergalactic Brotherhood of Light), and God-realized humans.

Star councils: Coordinators and directors of multi-spatial, intergalactic business affairs. All aware galactic citizens have input upon the star councils. Arcturians in service to Earth sit upon the star councils as a subdivision of the Supreme Hierarchical Council for Planetary Ascension, System Sol, Intergalactic Brotherhood of Light.

Star grids: See *Grids.*

Stargate: A multidimensional access window. See the movies *2001: A Space Odyssey* and *Stargate* for a graphic portrayal of stargate dynamics.

Starseeds: Galactic beings on Earth as humans, animals, and plants. Many universes and star systems are represented, among them Arcturus, Pleiades, Sirius, and Orion.

Strands: See *Grids.*

Subconscious mind: The spirit mind, or intuitive heart-mind, that receives information from the superconscious, transforms it into symbols the brain-mind can understand, and then sends it to the brain-mind, or conscious mind.

Superconscious mind: The Soul mind, or higher Self mind. It uses the subconscious mind as a conduit to send information to the brain-mind, or conscious mind.

Vortex: Varying degrees of heightened energies that arise from a point along a grid where light strands crisscross. Vibration and light energy arising from a vortex varies greatly and may range from a few inches to miles. Intuitively, humans have always recognized vortices as power spots or sacred sites. Refer to Volume I, Part III for more detailed information.

Yin-yang: Ancient Chinese symbol used in the teachings of the Tao and the I Ching. Yin is feminine; yang is masculine. Yin-yang demonstrates all polarities and diversities (the ten thousand things) that exist within the universal whole.

Suggested Books and Movies

Books

Agartha: A Journey to the Stars. Meredith Lady Young-Sowers. Walpole, N.H.: Stillpoint, 1984.

Alchemy of the Human Spirit: A Guide to Human Transition into the New Age. Kryon (Spirit), [channelled by] Lee Carroll. Del Mar, Calif.: Kryon Writings, 1996.

Aliens Among Us. Ruth Shick Montgomery. New York: Fawcett, Crest, 1985.

An Act of Faith: Transmissions from the Pleiades. P'taah (Spirit), [channelled by] Jani King. The P'taah Tapes series. Cairns, Queensland, Australia: Triad, 1991; York Beach, Maine: Samuel Weiser, 1996.

Ancient America. Jonathan Norton Leonard. Great Ages of Man; A History of the World's Cultures series. (Nazca Lines.) New York: Time-Life Books, 1967.

Autobiography of a Yogi. Paramahansa Yogananda. Los Angeles: Self-Realization Fellowship, 1946.

Bashar: Blueprint for Change: A Message from Our Future. Bashar (Spirit), [channelled by] Darryl Anka. Edited by Luana Ewing. Seattle: New Solutions, 1990.

Beyond Ascension. Joshua D. Stone. Sedona, Ariz.: Light Technology Communication Services, 1995.

Beyond Stonehenge. Gerald S. Hawkins. New York: Harper & Row, 1973; New York: Marboro Books, Dorset, 1989.

The Book of Knowledge: The Keys of Enoch. J. J. Hurtak. Los Gatos, Calif.: Academy for Future Science, 1977.

Bringers of the Dawn: Teachings from the Pleiadians. Barbara Marciniak. Santa Fe, N.M.: Bear, 1992.

Celestial Raise: 'Tiers of Light' Pouring Fourth from the Son. Edited by Marcus. Mt. Shasta, Calif.: ASSK (Association of Sananda and Sanat Kumara), 1986.

The Complete Ascension Manual for the Aquarian Age. Joshua D. Stone. Sedona, Ariz.: Light Technology Communication Services, 1994.

The Crystal Stair: A Guide to the Ascension: Channeled Messages from Sananda (Jesus), Ashtar, Archangel Michael, and St. Germain. Eric Klein. Edited by Sara Benjamin-Rhodes. Livermore, Calif.: Oughten House, 1990; third edition, 1994.

The Divine Romance. Paramahansa Yogananda. Los Angeles: Self-Realization Fellowship, 1986.

Don't Think Like a Human!: Channelled Answers to Basic Questions. Kryon (Spirit), [channelled by] Lee Carroll. Del Mar, Calif.: Kryon Writings, 1994.

The Earth Chronicles series. Vols. I–V. Zecharia Sitchin. New York: Avon Books; Santa Fe, N.M.: Bear, 1980–1993.

Earth's Birth Changes. St. Germain (Spirit), [channelled by] Azena Ramada. St. Germain Series. Cairns, Queensland, Australia: Triad; York Beach, Maine: Samuel Weiser, 1996.

The End Times, New Information for Personal Peace: Channelled Teachings Given in Love. Kryon (Spirit), [channelled by] Lee Carroll. Del Mar, Calif.: Kryon Writings, 1992.

E.T. 101: The Cosmic Instruction Manual for Planetary Evolution. Mission Control (Spirit), [channelled by] Zoev Jho. San Francisco: HarperSanFrancisco, 1994. Originally published as channelled by Diana Luppi (1990).

The Findhorn Garden. Findhorn Foundation. New York: HarperCollins, 1975.

God I Am: Inspired by the Triad of Isis, Immanuel and St. Germain. Peter O. Erbe. Cairns, Queensland, Australia: Triad; York Beach, Maine: Samuel Weiser, 1996.

The Gods of Eden: A New Look at Human History. William Bramley. New York: Avon Books, 1989.

Hidden Mysteries. Joshua D. Stone. Sedona, Ariz.: Light Technology Communication Services, 1995.

Lazaris (Spirit) series books, videos, and cassettes. Palm Beach, Fla.: Visionary Publishing.

Life and Teachings of the Masters of the Far East. Vols. I–V. Baird T. Spalding. Marina del Rey, Calif.: DeVorss, 1924.

Mary's Message to the World: As Sent by Mary, the Mother of Jesus, to Her Messenger Annie Kirkwood. Mary, Blessed Virgin, Saint (Spirit), [channelled by] Annie Kirkwood. Edited by Brian Kirkwood. New York: Putnam, 1991; New York: Berkley, Perigee, 1996.

The Mayan Factor: Path Beyond Technology. Jose Arguelles. Santa Fe, N.M.: Bear, 1987.

The Monuments of Mars: A City on the Edge of Forever (book and video). Richard C. Hoagland. Berkeley, Calif.: North Atlantic Books, Frog, Ltd., 1987.

The Nature of Personal Reality: Specific, Practical Techniques for Solving Everyday Problems and Enriching the Life You Know (and other Seth series books). Seth (Spirit), [channelled by] Jane Roberts. Englewood Cliffs, N.J.: Prentice-Hall, 1974; San Rafael, Calif.: Amber-Allen, 1994.

Nothing in This Book Is True, But It's Exactly How Things Are: The Esoteric Meaning of the Monuments on Mars. Bob Frissell. Berkeley, Calif.: North Atlantic Books, Frog, Ltd., 1994.

The Only Planet of Choice: Essential Briefings from Deep Space. Phyllis V. Schlemmer and Palden Jenkins. Edited by Mary Bennett. Bath, England: Gateway; Lower Lake, Calif.: Atrium, 1993.

A Path with Heart: A Guide through the Perils and Promises of Spiritual Life. Jack Kornfield. New York: Bantam Books, 1993.

The Pleiadian Agenda: A New Cosmology for the Age of Light. Barbara Hand Clow. Santa Fe, N.M.: Bear, 1995.

Project World Evacuation: UFOs to Assist in the "Great Exodus" of Human Souls off this Planet. Compiled through Tuella by the Ashtar Command. Edited by Timothy Green Beckley. Petaluma, Calif.: Inner Light Publications, 1993.

Ramtha. Ramtha (Spirit), [channelled by] JZ Knight. Edited by Steven L. Weinberg. Bellevue, Wash.: Sovereignty, 1986.

The Star-Borne: A Remembrance for the Awakened Ones. Solara. Charlottesville, Va.: Star-Borne, 1989.

The Starseed Transmissions. Ken Carey. San Francisco: HarperSanFrancisco, 1991.

Surfers of the Zuvuya: Tales of Interdimensional Travel. Jose Arguelles. Santa Fe, N.M.: Bear, 1988.

The Third Millennium: Living in the Posthistoric World. Ken Carey. San Francisco: HarperSanFrancisco, 1995. Originally published as *Starseed, the Third Millennium* (1991).

The Tibetan Book of Living and Dying: A New Spiritual Classic from One of the Foremost Interpreters of Tibetan Buddhism to the West. Sogyal Rinpoche. San Francisco: HarperSanFrancisco, 1993.

Transformation of the Species: Transmissions from the Pleiades. Jani King. The P'taah Tapes series. Cairns, Queensland, Australia: Triad.

The Treasure of El Dorado: Featuring "the Dawn Breakers." Joseph Whitfield. Roanoke, Va.: Treasure, 1977; reprint, 1989.

UFOs and the Nature of Reality: Understanding Alien Consciousness and Interdimensional Mind. Ramtha (Spirit), [channelled by] JZ Knight. Edited by Judi Pope Koteen. Eastsound, Wash.: Indelible Ink, 1990.

We, the Arcturians. Norma J. Milanovich. Albuquerque, N.M.: Athena, 1990.

With Wings As Eagles: Discovering the Master Teacher in the Secret School Within. John R. Price. Boerne, Texas: Quartus Books, 1987; Carson, Calif.: Hay House, 1997.

You Are Becoming a Galactic Human. Washta (Spirit), [channelled by] Virginia Essene and Sheldon Nidle. Santa Clara, Calif.: SEE (Spiritual Education Endeavors), 1994.

Movies ("Management training films")

2001: A Space Odyssey. Stanley Kubrick film.

2010: The Year We Make Contact. Peter Hyams film.

Always. Steven Spielberg film.

Batteries Not Included. Steven Spielberg film.

Close Encounters of the Third Kind (extended version). Steven Spielberg film.

Cocoon. Ron Howard film.

Contact. Robert Zemeckis film.

Defending Your Life. Geffen Pictures.

Field of Dreams. P. A. Robinson film.

Ghost. Jerry Zucker film.

Heart and Souls. Ron Underwood film.

Heaven Can Wait. Paramount.

Hoagland's Mars. Richard C. Hoagland.

Made in Heaven. Lorimar Motion Pictures.

Shirley MacLaine's Inner Workout. High Ridge Productions.

Star Trek (entire series, both motion pictures and television, especially *Star Trek IV: The Voyage Home*).

Star Wars trilogy: *Star Wars, The Empire Strikes Back, Return of the Jedi.* George Lucus films.

Starman. John Carpenter film.

Willow. Ron Howard film.

THE ARCTURIAN STAR CHRONICLES SERIES

Patricia L. Pereira started receiving telepathic communications from the star Arcturus in 1987 and transcribed a message of hope and encouragement about the changes we will experience in the years to come. These galactically inspired pages have become the Arcturian Star Chronicles.

Volume One
Songs of the Arcturians
$12.95 softcover
Practical and uplifting cosmically inspired manual designed to assist the individual in preparing for galactic citizenship and matters pertaining to personal evolution.

Volume Two
Eagles of the New Dawn
$12.95 softcover
Galactic essays and exercises to assist awakening humans (eagles of the new dawn) in unlocking their soul memories and purposefully connecting with higher dimensional spirit energies.

Volume Three
Songs of Malantor
Available Fall 1998

Volume Four
Songs of the Masters of Light
Available Fall 1999

These titles are available through your local bookstore or from Beyond Words Publishing at 1-800-284-9673.